Pennsy Steam
and Semaphores

A locomotive of graceful lines surmounts a stone bridge of massive, yet artistic design. That was a Pennsylvania Railroad credo in days gone by. To Pennsy engineers something did not have to be cumbersome or ugly to be efficient. And how well they proved this concept in the fields of mechanical, civil, and signal engineering. Scene was on the Pittsburgh Division where the railroad crosses one of the many stone bridges that are a good part of it. Engine was hauling the Pennsy's official photographic car used by William H. Rau, of Philadelphia, when he made those splendid scenic views in 1892 and 1893. Note the white flags on front of engine indicating an ''extra'' train not listed in the public timetable.

Pennsy Steam
and Semaphores

by

FRED WESTING

BONANZA BOOKS • NEW YORK

Copyright © 1974 by Superior Publishing Company

This 1982 edition is published by Bonanza Books,
distributed by Crown Publishers, Inc., by arrangement with
Superior Publishing Company.

Manufactured in the United States of America

Library of Congress Cataloging in Publication Data

Westing, Fred, 1903–
    Pennsy steam and semaphores.
    Originally published: Seattle : Superior
Pub. Co., 1974.
    Includes index.
    1. Locomotives—United States.   2. Railroads—
United States—Signaling.   3. Pennsylvania
Railroad.   I. Title.
TJ603.3.P46W47   1982   625.2′61′0974   81-18178
                                                    AACR2

ISBN: 0-517-369559

h   g   f   e   d   c   b   a

To the memory of my parents Thomas and Louise Westing who encouraged my interest in locomotives and railroads.

Contents

Preface

While this book is not a history of the Pennsylvania Railroad or its locomotives, it does concentrate on informative sidelights generally ignored or unknown regarding these subjects.

In most books written about the Pennsy and its locomotives, it appears that there is a lamentable omission of train scenes taken in the period between the 1890's up to the late 1920's. To rectify this situation is a primary function of this publication. For in it will be found some rare vintage pictures of Pennsy train scenes with authentic "in depth" captions to cover them.

Although passenger train scenes and locomotives predominate, there is a Chapter covering freight trains and locomotives taken during the era referred to.

No locomotives designed after 1919 are illustrated, with two exceptions, one G5s class, 4-6-0 type engine, and one M1 class Mountain type locomotive, both of which were designed after 1920. Pictures of Pennsy trains and locomotives from the 1930's on are legion, but illustrations of such material in volumes prior to 1930 are not found in any other one hard cover book...

In the Chapter "Facts and Figures" there will be found much of technical interest. It contains coal consumption records of Pennsy light Atlantics on specific runs in 1908, as well as showing the long distances that could be made by these engines without using fuel. Also included are some typical runs taken from a report made that year during an investigation conducted by four Pennsy engine service employees regarding the practicability of long distance runs over 200 miles with one engine and crew.

My object in identifying the classes of locomotives, and even many passenger cars is due to the fact that future historians and railbuffs may wish to pursue their own investigation concerning such equipment. This information could, therefore, provide a good starting point, and end in gratifying results.

Concluding, I would like to point out the reason for referring to the early Pennsy Atlantics as "light." As Professor Albert Einstein indicated many years ago, it is only by comparison that we differentiate between size. Thus it is only when we compare the so-called light Atlantics with the larger boilered and heavier E6s class Atlantics that we consider them as light or small. In their time the Pennsy's smaller boilered Atlantics were actually big power, and proved it often with big-sized performances.

Chapter 1
As the Century Ended

On the Pennsylvania Railroad in the 1890's, the brunt of passenger train operation was borne by locomotives of the American 4-4-0 type. This wheel arrangement had long been established on most American railroads, and as trains grew heavier and schedules speedier the American type was merely made larger and more powerful to meet those newer conditions.

During most of the 19th century's last decade, class P was the Pennsy's most advanced design of this type. Contemporary with class P, was class O, another 4-4-0 type locomotive. Both classes worked passenger trains on the Philadelphia Division. On the Middle Division between Harrisburg and Altoona, class O was a fixture in high-speed passenger service. West of Pittsburgh class O was used on the best trains as were some ten-wheelers of the 4-6-0 type. Originally class X, and later class G3, with 68″ drivers, they also worked top-name trains, and frequently headed, the Pennsylvania Limited. This class made its appearance in road service in 1893, when they were built.

Class P did exceptionally fine work on the two-hour trains between New York and Philadelphia. Here they duplicated speed made by trains fifty years later. This does not mean that progress was not made, for train loads of the nineties were comparatively light with 300 tons considered very heavy, while 130 tons was about the average train weight. It should be pointed out that while locomotives were much larger in later years, trains were correspondingly heavier. Average train loads ran from 600 to 800 tons, and trains exceeding 1,000 tons frequently made the schedules with power in reserve, while the old locomotives of the nineties with their much lighter loads were pushed to the limit of their power.

Among the name trains in the decade of the 1890's and early twentieth century, was one of the oldest named trains in the United States. It was known as the "Fast Line" and ran between New York and Pittsburgh. This name was derived from the Pioneer Fast Line which operated in the 1830's, and by means of railroad and canal boat transportation conveyed passengers and freight between Philadelphia and Pittsburgh in 3½ days. Another fine train in the 1890's was the Pennsylvania Limited, originated in 1881 as the New York & Chicago Limited.

In 1893 a large addition was made to the original Broad Street Station building. This new building was designed by Furness, Evans & Co. architects of Philadelphia. The first Broad Street Station building was designed and built by Wilson Brothers of Philadelphia. This was the section that included the distinctive clock tower at the northern end of the station. Opened in December 1881, it made connection with the main line in West Philadelphia by means of an elevated multi-tracked structure known for many years to Philadelphians as the Chinese Wall. A four-tracked steel bridge, also the work of Wilson Brothers & Co. carried trains across the Schuylkill River.

Preceding classes O and P, but doing much work in the 1890's was a locomotive introduced on the road in 1881. Known as class K, it represented high efficiency for that day. Of a group of eighteen the first one was No. 10, and engineer John A. Covert, who later became Road Foreman of Engines, of the New York Division, brought engine 10 from Altoona to that division in June 1881. Engine No. 10 was quickly named "long legged Ten" due to its high-wheeled 78 inch drivers, accentuated in great part by the seemingly small boiler. This engine with its general cleanlined appearance and omission of the former gingerbread mouldings seen on most locomotives in those days possessed unusual symmetry for an American locomotive.

On class K the firebox was placed on top of the main frames which made it shallow at the throat sheet. Subsequently all Pennsy standard 4-4-0's, provided for a deeper firebox throat by inclining the top main frame rails downwardly at the front.

A novel feature on class K was the use of a power reverse gear. This was a desirable detail on a locomotive using 140 lb. steam pressure with unbalanced slide valves. The combined use of steam and oil which locked the gear in any desired position was operated by a small lever in the cab. While reliable in service, it was abandoned when balanced slide valves came into use.

An interesting comparison was made between engine No. 10, and No. 724, one of the older engines of class A (later class D1) is listed below:

Class	Engine No.	Cylinders	Drivers, dia.	Pressure	Coal used per car mile
K	10	18″ × 24″	78″	140 lb.	8.32 lb.
A	724	17″ × 24″	68″	130 lb.	12.76 lb.

During the week ending June 18, 1881, the car mileage of engine No. 10 was 7,209 miles and, therefore, the total consumption of coal was 7,209 × 8.32 equals 59,978.8 lbs. If we take the same car mileage for engine No. 724, we would have a coal consumption of 7,209 × 12.76 equals 91,986.8 lbs., or a saving in one week of 91,986.8 minus 59,978.8 equals 32,008 lbs. by engine No. 10.

Both engines were of the 4-4-0 type, but class K was, as shown, indicative of progressive development as compared with Pennsy 4-4-0 American type engines that preceded it.

Class K was the work of Theodore N. Ely, then Superintendent of Motive Power at Altoona, and from 1893 to 1911, Chief of Motive Power of the Pennsylvania Railroad east and west of Pittsburgh. Mr. Ely's artistic ability was responsible for much of class K's uncluttered lines, and Axel Vogt, his ever capable Mechanical Engineer at Altoona, ably assisted him in this approach to locomotive construction by his meticulous attention to the design of many of the engine's details.

To show the speed capabilities of these class K locomotives, two instances can be cited. On March 10, 1890, Albert M. Palmer's Madison Square Theatre Company, traveled on a three-car special train from New York to Washington, D.C. The occasion was to provide a performance of the play "Aunt Jack" which many Washingtonians were anxious to see.

Over the New York Division the original K class engine No. 10, rushed the train to Philadelphia (Grays Ferry) in considerably less than two hours, averaging about 57 mph. for the entire distance. From that point class P engine No. 35, similar in many respects to class K, but with 68″ drivers, made the run to Washington in 2 hours and 35 minutes, averaging nearly 60 mph. start-to-stop. Considering the fact that this latter part of the trip was double-tracked only, for a considerable distance, and traffic so heavy that several slow downs had to be made, commendable credit is due the train dispatchers and engine crew on this more difficult and lengthier part of the run.

Mr. Palmer had stipulated with the railroad that at the conclusion of the Washington performance, his theatrical group would have to immediately return to New York as they were committed to present an eight o'clock performance that evening in New York City. Again classes P and K gave their "performance" and the show that same evening made its scheduled appearance.

Prior to this run another K class locomotive No. 958, with engineer Joseph Fehr at the throttle hauled President Garfield's four-car Special train all the way from Washington, D.C., to Elberon, N.J. Here, it was hoped, the severely wounded President would recover from the attempt made upon his life in the Washington railroad station. But sad to relate it was not to be, and No. 958, a New York Division engine, had the mournful task on September 21,1881, of hauling the four-car Special with the remains of the President of the United States. The time for this southbound journey was 6 hours and 41 minutes. On both runs this train ran via Monmouth Junction and Sea Girt, N.J., and by this route made connection with the New York Division.

"Long legged ten" as it came from Altoona. Put into road service on March 25, 1881, this was the pioneer of the famous "K" class. With their 78 inch drivers they were real high-wheelers, and could make good speed (see text). Later, these locomotives had extended smokeboxes with the headlight supported on top of it.

Before we leave class K, another run worthy of mention is herewith given. On Saturday November 28, 1891, a special train carrying a party of guests to the opening of a new hotel in Washington, D.C., ran from Jersey City to Washington in 4 hours and 11 minutes. The 227 miles were covered in 240 minutes.

Class K engine No. 340, of the New York Division, took the train to Grays Ferry, Philadelphia, where five minutes were taken to change engines. This train left Jersey City at 2.49 pm., and passed Trenton 56 miles distant in 53 minutes, averaging over 60 mph., which included a 30 mph. speed restriction through the city of Newark, N.J., where the railroad ran at street level at the time. From Gray's Ferry to Washington, engine No. 181 of the Philadelphia, Wilmington & Baltimore Railroad Co., with engineer W. J. Hukill, headed the three-car train which consisted of a dining car, a parlor car named "Cecilia" and an observation parlor car named "Olympic." The weight of the cars was 125 tons and the locomotive and tender about 76½ tons. South of Philadelphia the engine of the P class had a hard time for there was a heavy continuous rain to Washington. Engine No. 181 made it from Philadelphia to Washington in 2 hours and 32 minutes, despite an unexpected six minute loss at Baltimore due to an equipment failure on one of the cars. The running time exclusive of stops was 56¾ mph.

On October 21, 1892 some test runs took place when three experimental locomotives and a class K standard Pennsy American type, ran in competition with each other over the New Jersey meadows between Jersey City and Newark. Each train pulled two cars, and the results were as follows:

One engineer well qualified to pass judgment on this matter remarked that "These engines were in no condition to make such test runs and made a fizzle of the affair."

A brief description of these locomotives is in order. No. 1504 was built at the Schenectady Locomotive Works (Alco) in 1892, and was a non-compound or simple engine. Engine No. 1510 was a four-cylinder Vauclain compound built by Baldwin in 1892. After running several years it was converted into a two-cylinder single-expansion, or simple non-compound locomotive in which fashion it ended its days. Both Nos. 1504 and 1510 were retired in 1911.

Engine 1320 was a Webb three-cylinder compound with two outside high-pressure cylinders and one low-pressure cylinder between them. It was built by Beyer, Peacock & Co. Ltd. of Manchester, England, in 1889 for experimental purposes. This locomotive represented a system of compound steam distribution devised by Francis W. Webb, then Locomotive Superintendent of the former London & North Western Railway of England. Engine 1320 was found to be too light and puny for the Pennsy, and four cars seemed to be its limit in passenger service. The meagre English cab was on the locomotive for awhile, but engine crews found it quite uncomfortable with its inadequate protection.

Three other compounds were built in 1892, beside 1504 and 1510, making five in all; one by Baldwin No. 1502, of the 4-6-0 type using the four-cylinder Vauclain compound arrangement, and the other, No. 1503 a two-cylinder cross compound also a 4-6-0 type ten-wheeler built by Schenectady. But a more interesting and even spectacular 4-4-0 type engine No. 1515 a two-cylinder cross compound was this "home product" built at Altoona in 1892.

Class	Type	Engine	Fastest time per mile	Speed, mph.	Engineer
Odd	440	1504	54 seconds	66.6	George Headden
Odd	440	1510	56 seconds	64.3	John A. Covert
Odd	240	1320	65 seconds	55.3	John W. Hartman
K	440	340	48 seconds	75.0	George Roe

It was known as class T, (later D15) and was of unusual design. Newspaper accounts of the day hailed it as "The One Hundred Miles An Hour Engine." Oil was to be used for fuel but before going on the road bituminous coal was decided upon for fuel.

Axel S. Vogt, Mechanical Engineer of the Pennsy at Altoona, was the designer of this locomotive. Mr. Vogt became Mechanical Engineer of the Pennsy on March 1, 1887, and on February 1, 1919, in accordance with Company policy he retired, having reached 70 years of age. He was succeeded by William F. Kiesel, Jr., who ably carried on the Pennsy's tradition as exponents of highly efficient steam locomotive design combined with a noticeable regard for external appearance.

Engine No. 1515 in its appearance showed strong British Railway influence. Wheel splashers or covers and running board gives the impression that the London & North Western Railway motif of the Webb compound was appropriated by No. 1515. A rigid six-wheel tender with 42 inch locomotive truck and tender wheels showed a distinct departure from standard American practice.

The outstanding feature of this locomotive was its use of the Lindner two-cylinder cross compound system of delivering steam to the cylinders. This method was the invention of Herr Lindner, an engineer from Saxony in Germany. It was known as a semi-automatic system and was much less complicated than other compound arrangements.

When starting a train the locomotive was put into full gear and worked single expansion. This gave a cut-off of 78.6 per cent of the stroke in the high-pressure cylinder which was located on the left side of the locomotive. On the right side, steam at a cut-off of 83.9 per cent of the stroke fed steam to the low-pressure cylinder. Piston valves $12\frac{1}{2}$ inches in diameter placed in line with the two cylinders were used.

In 1895 old locomotive classifications were changed by using one letter to designate different classes having specific wheel arrangements. Thus the American, 4-4-0 type became class D with numerals representing modifications and progressive development in general.

For what were considered experimental locomotives after 1895, the Pennsy appeared to start with the numeral 28 after a certain class letter. In this way they had classes E28, and E29, the H28, and K28 and K29. They probably concluded that further developments, and consequently numerals, would have stopped on that particular class long before reaching number 28, and thus prevent a duplication of classes when consistently using a strictly numerical sequence arrangement.

Meanwhile old class P steadily increased in size and power finally reaching its pinnacle in the D16 class and its subsequent sub-classes. Engine No. 88, was bulit in the then quite new Juniata shops in 1895, and pioneered the first of this illustrious clan which finally numbered 429 units.

Engine 88 must have been completed before the new classification system became official—some records list it as 1897 rather than 1895. Anyway, No. 88 was first recorded as class P in 1895, but in 1896, it became class L. In 1897 No. 88 became D16a class engine of the American type. It was brought to the New York Division by engineer John Wesley (Wes) Hartman, and fireman John Sankey, employees of this Division. Engine No. 88 often hauled the Congressional Limited between Jersey City and West Philadelphia, Pa.

Soon after other engines of class D16a came on the road as well as several sub-classes known as D16, D16b, D16c, and D16d. In 1914 the first engine of the D16 group was equipped with a superheater, namely engine No. 178, class D16b which then became class D16sb, of the New York Division, and soon numerous others of class D16b were so equipped as were those of class D16a which had their 80 inch drivers replaced with 68 inch driving wheels as used on class D16b when built. On the railroad west of Pittsburgh class D16d appeared to be used for fast passenger service, but the other engines of this group ran plentifully on the road east of Pittsburgh. Some D16d class engines did, however, operate east of Pittsburgh. One, in particular did some fine work on the old West Jersey and Seashore Railroad. Table No. 1 lists four speedy runs made by engine No. 5, class D16d, of the WJ&S Railroad. A more detailed record of the run made on August 15, 1900, is shown on table No. 2. This as can be seen was made by an observer who rode the engine. His comments regarding the assistance given to the fireman by the engineer are of interest.

Engine No. 317 representing another engine of class K. These engines unlike most in this country omitted the sandbox on top of the boiler. Instead two sandboxes were placed under the running boards—one per side—and inside the front wheel covers, or splashers as British railwaymen call them. Just outside the cab can be seen the power reverse gear that was actuated (see text) by steam and oil.

Years ago when railroad transportation represented the speediest form of land travel—and still does—newspapers used to record some fast runs and other exceptional news made by trains. Especially was this so in railroad cities like Altoona and Harrisburg, when the Harrisburg "Patriot" in July 1900, reported as follows; "Train No. 13, of the Pennsylvania Railroad, on July 26, made the run from Harrisburg to Altoona, 132 miles, at the rate of 41.9 miles an hour, including 33 stops. The train left Harrisburg 43 minutes behind time and reached Altoona five minutes ahead of time. The train was made up of postal cars, a combination car, and three passenger coaches. It was hauled by engine 492, (class D16a built at Juniata Shops in 1897-FW.) and was in charge of engineer William Kurtz and Conductor J. S. Wagner. From Bailey's to Newport, a distance of five miles, the running time was four minutes."

Considering that the Middle Division which is between Harrisburg and Altoona has a predominantly ascending grade when running westbound, this was a highly creditable performance. To make up time on a run while making 33 stops on an uphill grade called for a skilled hand on the throttle, and a mighty good fireman. Such a run put more pressure on an engine crew than a non-stop run with the Pennsylvania Limited over a division.

But despite the fine work of the D16 group, the 4-4-0 type engines began to find themselves outclassed. For the Philadelphia & Reading which operated the Atlantic City Railroad, had obtained two splendid performing Atlantics of the 4-4-2 type. These engines Nos. 1026 and 1027, made railroad history. Both were Vauclain four-cylinder compounds built by Baldwin in March 1896.

How the Pennsy reacted to this situation, and came to adopt the Atlantic for passenger service everywhere on their railroad is the subject of the next Chapter.

Table No. 1   Table of runs made by D16d class engine No. 5 on the West Jersey and Seashore Railroad

Date	Engine class	Engine No.	Train No.	Number of cars	Train weight	From	To	Number of miles and time	Average speed MPH.	Passengers per trip
July 14, 1899	D16d	5	257	6	612,280 lb.	Pomona	Drawbridge	11.2 miles 8 mins.	84	262
Aug. 3, 1899	D16d	5	257	5	557,800 lb.	Winslow Junction	Egg Harbor	14.3 miles 10½ mins.	81	230
Aug. 15, 1899	D16d	5	250	5	573,000 lb.	Lucaston	Haddonfield	7 miles 4½ mins.	93	185
Sept. 18, 1899	D16d	5	635	7	649,150 lb.	West Haddonfield Atco	Atlantic City Absecon	52 miles 45 mins. 39.19 miles 27 mins.	70 73.1	77

This engine was a class P (later D11a) of 1883 design and externally was much like class K. Exceptions were the 68 inch drivers and larger cylinders. As with class K, no sandbox originally appeared on the boiler, but later in the 1890's, classes K, O, and P, (all American 4-4-0 types) had their sandboxes and wheel covers removed and placed a dome type sandbox on top of the boiler. Class P fitted into the most difficult high-speed passenger service with notable success on the New York Division and some other locations where hard coal was used. They also proved most capable in freight service when called upon. A versatile type that 4-4-0 wheel format! The engine illustrated belonged to the Philadelphia, Wilmington & Baltimore Railroad, the old P.W.&B. Road number was 115, and it was built at Altoona in 1887, shop number 1149.

Christmas day in 1908, a D11a class engine No. 728 of 1886 vintage from Altoona, shop number 1054, heads a train on the Bustleton Branch. Picture was taken at the Bustleton end of the line. This train ran to Holmesburg Junction where it made connection with the main line of the New York Division. By 1908 it was standard practice to put the air pump on the left side of the locomotive. Note the old wooden coaches with tanks under the coach body for the storage of gas for lighting the cars.

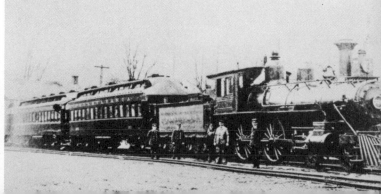

Mileage		Due. h. m.	Running h. m. s.	
	Atlantic City, dep....	8 0	8 0 10	
1	Drawbridge, p.	8 2	8 2 10	(slow for drawbridge, 10 s.)
5·7	Abescon, p.	8 8	8 8 43	
5·5	Pomona, p.	8 12	8 13 30	
2·4	Germania, p.	8 14	8 15 30	
2·7	Egg Harbour, p.	8 16	8 17 38	
5	Elwood, p.	8 20	8 21 55	
4	Da Costa, p.	8 23	8 25 20	
2·1	Hammonton, p.	8 25	8 26 58	
3·2	Winslow Junct., p.	8 27	8 29 44	
2·3	Ancora, p.	8 29	8 31 37	
2	Waterford, p.	8 31	8 33 12	
3·7	Atco, p.	8 33	8 36 17	
2·6	Berlin, p.	8 35	8 38 30	5·1
	Kirkwood, p.			42, 42-3/5, 42-4/5.
4·6	Haddonfield, p.	8 43	8 45 50	
2·5	Collingswood, p.			
1·1	City Line, p.	8 47	8 48 30	(time lost, 1 m.)
2·8	Camden, arr.	8 53	8 52 20	

Loco.   5 (D-16a); standard 8-wheel type, 18½ × 26 cylinders,
        185 lbs. of steam.
Load: 5 cars, or 195 tons;
        1 compo. baggage car;
        1 parlour car;
        3 day cars.

					m.	s.
Running time booked		...	...	...	53	0
Running time taken		...	...	...	52	10
Slows	...	...	...	...	1	10
Net	...	...	...	...	51	0
Gain	...	...	...	...	2	0
Speed, m.p.h., 68.59	...	...	...	...	2	0

This is a splendid performance for the D-16 type of engine, which is very much smaller and less powerful than the E-1 class. No. 698 can take 3 more loaded coaches than this class. I have never seen a crew work better together, the way the driver helped the fireman in firing by swinging the fire-box door open and shut to prevent cold air rushing in was excellent.

A most successful group of engines of the P class were those later given a D11a classification. And one of the best among these was engine No. 1063. This locomotive operated over the Philadelphia Division in the 1890's where it frequently hauled the Pennsylvania Limited, the road's top-name train of the day. The pipe connected to the top of the steam dome was the Ashton blow-back safety valve. The object of this arrangement was to feed the escaping steam back to the tender tank. Later the pipe just ran to the cab roof, thence tapped into a muffler of Pennsy design. It remained a standard on the road for several years. The manually operated lever for the water scoop was on the right hand side of the tender, and the scoop can be seen between the two tender trucks.

Engine No. 351, class O, built at Altoona in 1889. This class did most of its running on the Philadelphia and Middle Divisions. Here they were regularly coupled to the Pennsylvania Limited and easily maintained the required schedule on both east and westbound runs.

Interior view of the Jersey City trainshed. From here passengers took ferryboats to Manhattan Island and Brooklyn. The baggage trucks on the third platform from the left were typical at this terminal. Despite the comparatively small boilers of the locomotives, their ability to generate steam was phenomenal. Picture was taken about 1893. Wooden cars which were lighted by gas are in prolific evidence.

A low-wheeled American type engine of class P, hauling a two-car local near Baltimore. Old style lower quadrant signals governed train movements.

The original Broad Street Station and building opened on December 5, 1881. The cost of the station and the Chinese Wall elevated structure plus the four-tracked bridge across the Schuylkill River, totaled $4,272,000, a tidy sum indeed for those days. But it brought the Pennsy directly into the center of Philadelphia directly opposite the City Hall, which building is still in use. Out in the yard can be seen 17th street tower, later replaced by tower "A". Filbert Street to the right, or north faces the railroad. This original station building was designed by Wilson Bros. Civil Engineers of Philadelphia. The clock tower at the right lasted until the end of Broad Street Station's existence.

Engine No. 1178, class P, waits on the elevated structure near Broad Street Station in the 1890's. Engine is on north side of the "Chinese Wall" with houses on adjoining Filbert Street in background. Locomotive was waiting to back up and couple to an outgoing train.

Engineer Jim Mitchel in the cab of engine No. 10, of the old P class, later class D13c. This "ten spot" ran on the West Jersey & Seashore Railroad and was built at Altoona in 1893. It is not to be confused with No. 10, of old class K, which operated on the New York Division and had its number appropriated in 1908 by an engine of the E3d class. This latter engine was quite a favorite and was of the Atlantic type, of which more later.

An O class engine heads train No. 5, the westbound Pennsylvania Limited for Chicago as it prepares for departure from the original Broad Street Station, in 1892. Engine was No. 1395, and took the train over the Philadelphia Division to Harrisburg. There, most likely, another class O engine took over for the river grade run to Altoona. Class O, after 1895, when a new classification system went into effect, became class D10a. Engine No. 1395 had its number given to a class D16a engine in 1898.

Class G3 was a powerful ten-wheeler numbered 7273. With 68 inch drivers it was built for passenger service on the PFW&C RR. in December, 1892. Originally numbered 273, engines of this class built at the Fort Wayne Shops, hauled the Pennsylvania Limited and other fast trains on the Fort Wayne route. They developed higher tractive force than the latest P class engines at the time, and carried more weight on drivers.

Only two of these G3a class engines were built, and with their 62 inch drivers, were usually employed in freight service on the PFW&C line of Pennsy Lines West. Engine No. 7279 was built at Fort Wayne Shops, April 1893. At that time it was designated as class X, and carried road number 279. Both classes G3 and G3a, had a ventilator of the clerestory or monitor type on their cab roofs. This was a standard feature on Lines West locomotives.

On April 21, 1895, a special one-car train left Camden Terminal as illustrated bound for Atlantic City 58.3 miles to the seashore. Engine No. 1658, class D14, made the run with combination car No. 5116 in 45¾ minutes, averaging 76.46 mph. From Liberty Park to Absecon, 49.18 miles the running time was 37½ minutes, and average speed 79.7 mph; from Berlin to Absecon 35.6 miles running time was 25¾ minutes, average speed 82.9 mph. From Winslow Junction to Absecon 24.9 miles, running time was 16 minutes, average speed 83 mph. The fastest mile was made in 41 seconds at a speed of 87.8 mph. Tom Bodell, who later became Road Foreman of Engines on the West Jersey & Seashore Railroad, was the engineer. Superintendent A. O. Dayton who rode the train took the leaving time at Camden, and at all stations on the line. Time between mileposts was taken by Supervisor D. F. Vaughan, and J. H. Nichol, Assistant Engineer, with the former calling the mileposts and the latter recording the time.

Engine No. 1659, which returned to the 78 inch drivers as used on old class K. There were six of these engines built at Altoona in July 1893. Known as class P of 1893 (later D14 class) they were numbered as follows; 1658, 1659, and 1660 for the New York Division, while Nos. 225, 226, and 227, went to the Philadelphia, Baltimore & Washington Division. These locomotives had Krupp wheels on their engine trucks made in Essen, Germany. Engine No. 1660, was reputed to be the first to have brakes for the engine truck wheels. A trap door ventilator was used, and the air pump was placed on the left side of the engine. A muffler was placed in the front end over the exhaust nozzle. With their 78 inch drivers they had speed a'plenty, and all-in-all, represented a fine example of railroad mechanical engineering. Martin Lee, often with Flavel Smith his fireman whom Lee considered to be one of the best, and who later became a top-notch steam locomotive engineer, had one or the other of the three New York Division engines on the "Owl" which left Jersey City at 12:30 a.m. and arrived at Broad Street Station at 3.35 a.m.

Largest 4-4-0 type in the country was this Lindner two cylinder cross-compound locomotive No. 1515, when built in 1892 at Altoona. British influence can be seen in the low running boards and wheel splashers. Six-wheel tender with a rigid wheelbase also indicates this. Possibly the Motive Power Department at Altoona, may have been motivated by the neat appearance of the Webb compound engine No. 1320, in this action. Picture was quite likely taken at Waldo Avenue enginehouse, in Jersey City. Square case headlight later replaced the original round cased design. Cylinder on left side (see text) used live, or high-pressure steam. To reduce weight as much as possible machinery details were carefully worked out. Eye beam sections were used for the main and side rods, and a crosshead of light under-hung design was used. With the piston valves between the cylinders, they were driven directly from the links and dispensed with rocker arms. After some break-in runs some changes were made in the front end to improve the steaming, after which the engine went into service on the New York Division.

The **"One Hundred Miles-an-Hour Engine"**, No. 1515, at high speed near Linden, N.J. in the summer of 1897, with the seven car eastbound section of the Pennsylvania Limited, as its seven-foot driving wheels rapidly cover ground. Engine still retained round-cased headlight at the time. Train consist is in reverse order as Observation-Compartment-Sleeping Car which was last car on train when leaving Chicago is coupled to engine tender. This was due to train running via Broad Street Station, Philadelphia, a stub, or dead-end terminal. New York Division locomotive, in this instance, and in fact quite regularly, No. 1515, the Lindner compound, then coupled to the last car entering the station which reversed the train consist and put the Combination-Baggage Car at the train's rear end.

A typical consist of wooden Pullman cars used on this train as shown here with their authentic names at this time could well have been as follows:

Observation-Comp't. Sleeper	ALROY
Sleeper	ORLEANS
Sleeper	PARAGON
Sleeper	PELION
Sleeper	ETRURIA
Dining Car	ABERLIN
Parlor-Baggage Car	PREMIER

While this locomotive did some good work it failed to show marked superiority over Pennsy standard passenger locomotives. Two cylinder cross-compounds were considered better applied to freight service. Unbalanced forces between the high-pressure and low-pressure sides of the locomotive created maintenance problems in high-speed operation; consequently engine No. 1515, had a short life span. On December 20, 1895, engine 1515, hauled the seven-car Pennsylvania Limited eastbound over the New York Division, from Broad Street Station to Jersey City in 105 minutes. Engineer was J. Niece.

A Pennsy D16a beauty of 1895. Last of the class P engines in line of development. This was one of the finest, neatest and most efficient American 4-4-0 type engines to grace the rails. In 1896 became known as class "L." By 1897 the new classification system became standardized and class L became class D16a. The first locomotive of class D16a was No. 88, and engineer John Wesley "Wes" Hartman with fireman John Sankey, were sent to Altoona to fetch her back east to the New York Division where they were employed. From the start No. 88 did a great job for the trains of that day. In a special test run a train of seven of the heaviest Pullman cars simulating the Pennsylvania Limited in their consist, was speeded 89.6 miles from Jersey City to Broad Street, Philadelphia in 99¾ minutes at an average speed of 53.88 mph. Wes Hartman was the engineer, and he had engine No. 1651, class D16a at the head end. This was an excellent feat considering the fact that one of the wooden Pullman cars named PARAGUAY the heaviest of them all weighed alone 115,200 lb. while the total train weight was 434.31 tons. Engine No. 101 as shown here was a D16a similar to No. 88 and No. 1651. It was built at the Juniata Shops in 1895.

A westbound passenger train hauled by engine No. 296, class D16a. This was the first engine of this class on the Philadelphia Division, and frequently hauled the Pennsylvania Limited.

 "AMERICA'S GRANDEST RAILWAY TERMINAL"
— PENNSYLVANIA RAILROAD —
NEW PASSENGER STATION. BROAD STREET. PHILADELPHIA. U.S.A.

The new Broad Street Station building was an addition to the old building, thereby, completely covering the space between Filbert Street and Market Street to the south. Architects for this extension were Furness, Evans & Co. of Philadelphia. Pennsy President, George B. Roberts, made the proposal that a larger building be built adjoining the older station and utilize the "air rights" for more office space. This was done, and the handsome Victorian Gothic structure and tall tower were the result. Later, the roof of the old (1881) building was changed to a flattened form which provided extra office space. This new addition was opened in November, 1893, as was a new huge steel trainshed that accommodated 16 tracks which if stretched in a single line would measure two miles in length. I recall the two lifts (usually called "elevators" in the U.S.) which ran between the street and train floors. There was also one in the big tower building on Market Street and wondered what the "E" floor stood for, until I saw it was marked Entresol, which was a sort of mezzanine or intermediate floor. This was the only office building in many cities where I ever saw that French word used to describe a mezzanine floor.

20

A doubleheader of two Americans climbing around the Horseshoe Curve as they work their westbound train. Railroad was still only double-tracked at this point. Leading engine was No. 134, class D16a, built at Juniata in 1897.

This D16a locomotive No. 225, was built at Juniata Shops in 1896. A few years were to pass before the word PENNSYLVANIA was to appear on the sides of the tender tank. Note the gold-leaf lettering and striping, even to the spokes of the engine's wheels. Two air drums were placed right in back of the smokebox saddle. Tender had the flared collar long associated with this type of locomotive.

A class D16c engine No. 5167 built at Altoona in 1899, shop number 2068, with a southbound express for Washington. Locomotive was assigned to the Maryland Division and was later converted to a D16sb class still operating in the 1920's.

Engine 926 built at Juniata Shops in 1897, heads a Schuylkill Division express train in West Philadelphia. A parlor car was in the consist of this train.
Picture at top of facing page shows this train in the Pennsy's West Philadelphia coach yards.

A **D16a** in West Philadelphia yards is backing this Schuylkill Division train into Broad Street Station. The appearance of P70 class all-steel coaches to the left would indicate the date to be somewhere between 1908 and 1910. The two door Adams express car is an interesting nostalgic item. The Adams Express Company, incidentally, did a fine job in the expeditious movement of such traffic.

A **class D16d** engine No. 227 built at Altoona Shops in 1901, for the former Philadelphia, Wilmington & Baltimore Railroad. Photo was taken in Philadelphia. Engine was later renumbered 5227, to conform to new numbering system on Maryland Division.

This train was known as the "Prince Henry of Prussia Special." Prince Henry was the brother of the German Kaiser, and his visit to the United States was something in the way of a diplomatic mission. He was well received, and on several occasions rode the cab of the engine hauling the Special train, an experience he thoroughly enjoyed. Scene was at Waldo Avenue Yard, in Jersey City, where passenger cars were stored and trains made up. At this point was also located a large round-house. Two tracks at extreme left were the main line New York Division passenger tracks, as the freight tracks diverted some distance west of this point, and ran to Harsimus Cove north of the passenger tracks and terminal in Jersey City. Train was composed of eight wooden Pullman cars, and date was May 1902. Cars in following order from engine were:

Combination-Smoking-Baggage Car	UTOPIA
Sleeping Car	BISCAY
Sleeping Car	GARONNE (For train attendants)
Dining Car	WILLARD
Compartment Sleeping Car	INDIANA
Compartment Sleeping Car	IOWA
Compartment Sleeping Car	OHIO
Observation-Comp't.-Sleeping Car	COLUMBIA (Car used by Prince Henry)

The car UTOPIA contained a steam turbine electric-generator set in that car's baggage compartment, and provided electricity for train lighting. An attendant (as on the Pennsylvania Limited) rode this car from Jersey City to Pittsburgh, and then, on trains to Chicago or St. Louis another man took over for the remainder of the run. Meanwhile the Jersey City man would return east on a car similarly equipped. The Dining Car WILLARD, was one of the latest built by Pullman, being splendidly fitted with all the newest equipment of a modern hotel both in the car's kitchen and dining section. Each Compartment Car had ten Staterooms in a row with a wide passage on one side from end-to-end of each such car. Prince Henry took his meals in the COLUMBIA where he entertained his numerous guests en route.

A close up of engine No. 631, which hauled the Prince from Jersey City over the New York Division. It was of the D16a class built at Juniata in 1898. Possibly as a gesture of good public relations, the engineer of this train was a native German who had served in that country's army before becoming an American citizen. He proudly displayed some medals he had obtained while in the army when his Royal Highness came up to greet the engine crew. The Prince, it was said graciously complimented the engineer upon their acquisition. Waldo Avenue yard was, it appears, open to the public that day to give anyone a chance for a good external view of this train. Note group of people to the right of the engine.

An E2 and a D16a approaching 34th Street bridge in West Philadelphia. First car is very old style baggage or express car of 1870 vintage. Train is No. 25, then called "The Fast Mail."

Crossing Bridge No. 69, the two-tracked deck truss that formerly spanned the Schuylkill River in Philadelphia, a D16a engine heads an eastbound New York "clocker" made up of wooden cars. First car is a Pullman, Parlor-Baggage car, then a Pullman, Parlor Car, followed by a Dining Car, and three open platform coaches. Date was 1904.

This picture of the famed Horseshoe Curve in color was one of many that appeared on the end of the south wall in the Penn Station arcade. Facing them were colored pictures on the North Wall. One showing an E3a engine hauling the Pennsylvania Special appears in a following Chapter of this book.

Engine No. 461, class D16d built at Altoona in 1900. The D16 class made up of 429 locomotives were the most prolific group of passenger engines ever owned by the Pennsylvania Railroad. They even exceeded the 425 class K4s engines, and all of them were built by the Pennsy at Altoona. No outside builder ever constructed one. In their day they were indeed, the Pennsy's pride and joy, and rightly so. The first D16 engine to arrive on the New York Division with injector check valves on the back-head when built, was No. 1433, class D16c, built in 1899 at Juniata. Later when engines of this group were converted to class D16sb, and some before, injector check valves were placed on their backheads. This eliminated side check valves on the boiler and lengthy outside piping.

The American type always had the reputation of being a versatile locomotive. High-speed passenger or freight service came within its field of operation. Here we see engine 5065, class D16b, with 68 inch drivers, built at Juniata in 1908 working a train of Fruit Growers Express "reefers," on the Maryland Division. These cars were painted colorfully in yellow and with the letters FGEX denoting their ownership on each end.

A Maryland Division D16a class engine. Arch bar trucks on the tender have given way to the Pennsy's own design of pedestal truck.

At Asbury Park, N.J., engine 593, class D16d, built at Altoona in 1900, heads an express train bound for New York. Photograph was probably taken before 1914, as old style injector checks with water delivery piping was still outside cab. Slide valve cylinders are also in use, but larger tender as used with light Atlantics has replaced original smaller sized tank. Train was on the New York & Long Branch Railroad, where Pennsy and Central Railroad of New Jersey Railroad tickets were interchangeable on the run to New York. Note open trap-door ventilator; picture was most likely taken during the summer season.

Chapter 2
Atlantics Meet the Challenge

In the free enterprise system, competition, like necessity, can at times be the mother of invention, and in the field of railroading has played its part in the design and construction of many locomotives.

We have seen in the previous Chapter that despite its speed prowess the best Pennsy American type locomotives were no match for the larger Reading Atlantics.

Passenger travel to the seashore was a most lucrative business eagerly sought for by the competing Pennsy and Reading. Without question, at the time the Reading had the upper hand. The two original Atlantics used on these runs were so satisfactory that the Reading ordered two more duplicates Nos. 1028 and 1029 from Baldwin to operate in the same service, and they were built in May 1898. All were of the four-cylinder Vauclain compound arrangement, and had driving wheels 84¼ inches in diameter. Specifically designed to cover the 55½ miles from Camden to Atlantic City in 60 minutes with eight cars, and 50 minutes with six cars, they speedily proved their ability to meet requirements. In fact, engine 1027 with Charley Fahl at the throttle hauling train No. 25, the Seashore Flyer broke records. This train soon became known and acknowledged as the World's fastest train. On August 5, 1898, engine 1027 hauled a six-car train from Camden to Atlantic City in 44¾ minutes at an average speed of 74.4 mph., while carrying 285 passengers. On one trip it was said No. 1027 hit a speed of 106 mph.

With understandable pride the Reading made the most of this and the speedy exploits of these four Atlantics were profusely publicized in pictures, and pamphlets. Even official operating records of these locomotives made from train dispatchers train sheets became available to the public.

Bluntly put, the Pennsy was up against it. They had nothing to match those four Reading Atlantics, and for "The Standard Railroad of the World" (an accolade well deserved in bygone days) to be outdone in this Atlantic City service was effrontery not to be borne!

But although the Reading had their Atlantics, the Pennsy had their Axel S. Vogt, railroad Mechanical Engineer extraordinary, and one of the greatest the railroad world has ever seen. Besides being an engineer Vogt was an accomplished linguist and could read the technical periodicals of France, Germany and Sweden, with equal facility. There was no phase of any form of railroad engineering with which he did not show exceptional knowledge. No one was better aware of Vogt's abilities than the astute Theodore N. Ely, Pennsy Chief of Motive power. Consequently he put Vogt to work on the design of an Atlantic type locomotive that would better the performance of the four Reading Atlantics.

In 1899 three Atlantics, Nos. 698, 700, and 820, class E1, of "Mother Hubbard" center cab, or "camelback" form were built for the summer service to the seashore at Atlantic City. These three engines represented splendid engineering and workmanship proving a credit to Vogt their designer and the Juniata Shops their builder.

Last of the three class E1 Atlantics. Three engines of this class were built in 1899, Nos. 698, 700, and 820. Designed by Axel S. Vogt, Pennsy Mechanical Engineer at Altoona, they showed their ability to match and even surpass the Reading's Atlantics. Pennsy did not, however, like the "camelback" arrangement that separated the engine crew despite the use of a speaking tube device that enabled the crew to communicate with each other. The rigid wheelbase of the six-wheel tender had a tendency to derail, and was not a popular feature of these otherwise fine locomotives.

First to arrive and go into service was No. 698. On June 20, 1899, when hauling train 46, the Washington & New York Limited Express, it was put to a hard test. Ten cars weighing 820,000 pounds, excluding engine and tender, made up of four Pullman cars, and six coaches, ran from Broad Street Station to Trenton, 33 miles, stopped, and left inside of 35 minutes. From Philadelphia to Jersey City, the 90 miles were covered in 109 minutes. This included two stops (Trenton and Newark) and three speed restrictions to scoop water from the track tanks which since 1874 had become a part of Pennsy operating procedure.

Engines 700 and 820 soon followed, and in time to handle the Philadelphia-Atlantic City traffic for which service they had been specifically built.

Expectations regarding their speed capabilities were not disappointing as can be seen by three officially recorded typical runs made in the summer of 1899.

July 23—Train No. 256, class E1 engine No. 698, 10 cars, 527 passengers, weight of train (not including passengers) 923,330 pounds. Elwood to Haddonfield 29.6 miles, in 24 minutes—74 mph. Berlin to Haddonfield, 9.7 miles, in 7 minutes—83.1 mph. Lucaston to Haddonfield, 7 miles, in 5 minutes—84 mph.

August 6—Train No. 256, class E1 engine No. 698, 11 cars, 518 passengers, weight of train (not including passengers) 987,950 pounds. Berlin to Collingswood, 12.2 miles in 9½ minutes—77 mph.

August 7—Train No. 256, class E1 engine No. 820, 7 cars, 264 passengers, weight of train (not

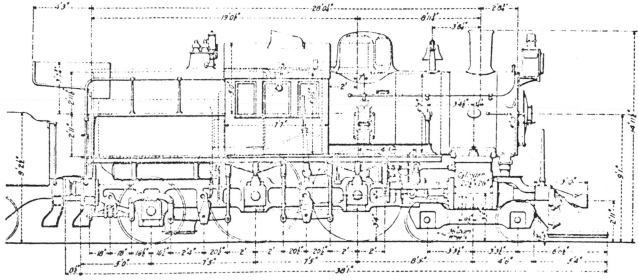

The New "Atlantic Type" Engine of the Pennsylvania Railroad—Class E-1, No. 698.

Diagram drawing of the first design of an Atlantic type locomotive on the Pennsylvania Railroad. From this design three engines were built at Juniata in 1899. After trial runs on the New York Division they went into regular service hauling trains between Philadelphia, Camden and Atlantic City. Here they made phenomenal high-speed runs in the summer of 1899.

Mileage.		Due. h. m.	Running. h. m. s.	
	Camden, dep. ...	5 5	5 7 12	(waiting for boat, slow out 15 s.)
3·9	Collingswood, p. ...		5 13 45	
2·5	Haddonfield, p. ...	5 14	5 16 15	
2·9	Ashland, p. ...	5 16	5 18 38	
1·7	Kirkwood ...		5 20 30	
2·4	Lucastown ...		5 22 40	
1·4	West Berlin, p. ...	5 21	5 24 3	
3·9	Atco, p. ...	5 24	5 27 30	
3·7	Waterford ...		5 30 25	
2	Ancora, p. ...		5 32 0	
2·3	Winslow Junct., p. ...		5 33 50	
3·2	Hammonton, p. ...	5 33	5 36 25	
2·1	Da Costa, p. ...	5 35	5 38 0	
4	Elwood, p. ...		5 41 12	
5	Egg Harbour, p. ...		5 45 7	
2·7	Germania, p. ...	5 44	5 47 16	
2·4	Pomona, p. ...	5 46	5 49 13	
5·5	Absecon, p. ...	5 52	5 53 28	(drawbridge slow at 5·57·40 for 15 s.)
6·7	Atlantic City, arr. ...	6 0	5 59 54	

Loco. 698 (E-1). Juniata shops, February 15, 1900. Belpaire box, 80-inch wheels, 20½ × 26 cylinders, non-compound.

Load : 8 cars, or 310 tons ;
    2 parlour cars ;
    5 day cars ;
    1 compo. baggage car.

						m.	s.
Running time booked	...	...	...	...		55	0
„ „ taken	...	...	...	...		52	42
Slacks	...	...	...	...	...		30
Net ...	...	...	...	...		52	12
Gain	...	...	...	...	...	2	48

Speed, m.p.h., 67·26.

This is one of the hardest trains to work between Camden and Atlantic City, as she is hardly ever off to time, owing to the very smart ferry connection, which barely allows enough time to get passengers and baggage into the train. This, however, hardly seems to matter, as, from what I learnt, a late arrival is an almost unknown occurrence. The day I went down on the engine we made up 2 min. 18 secs., including good slacks for the booked slows. We were hampered very much by a very nasty side head-wind. As it was a wide Belpaire fire-box, and I was on the left-hand side, I was not able to see how the driver handled the engine, but he did not seem to be working her up to her limit, and the fireman had no difficulty in keeping her steam steady. This is by no means one of the fastest runs that this engine has done, as, with an equal or greater load, her driver told me that she had gone down in 49 min. This train is very heavy, and is never less than 8, and often 9 or 10 coaches. The newest Pennsylvania loco., officially known as E-2, was unfortunately not long enough out of the shops to be running sufficiently cool to be put into regular fast work. She is an Atlantic City type, with a Belpaire box, non-compound. I have not seen her, but my friend says she is an exceptionally handsome engine. She is fast, as she took 14 loaded coaches down in 59 min. ; I have heard it said in 52 min.

Record of run made by E1 class engine No. 698 by an observer who was riding in the left side of the center cab. From this performance it is clear that Axel Vogt's locomotive had taken the play away from the Reading.

including passengers) 735,050 pounds, Winslow Junction to Doughty, 22.1 miles, in 16 minutes—82.8 mph.

It can be seen that although the D16d class engines equalled some of these records in speed, their train loads were considerably lighter. One E1 engine could handle a train that would require two trains or a doubleheader in order to accommodate an equivalent number of passengers while making the same schedule. Here was efficiency that produced economy, and clearly vindicated the Pennsy's approach to "fight fire with fire" for class E1 consistently hauled heavier loads at higher speeds than the rival Reading.

All these speeds made on the Pennsy by class E1, represent average speeds made between the points listed. Occasionally bursts of speed in the upper 90's were made which accounted for several of these high averages.

Despite the good performances of the three E1 locomotives, the Pennsy did not like the separation of the engine crew, although a novel method of communication was arranged between the engineer in the cab and the fireman on the tender deck. This was done by the use of a speaking tube fitted with the usual whistle mouthpiece. It was constantly used by the fireman by means of a conventional code whereby the engine crew could verbally double-check signals, long standard practice on the Pennsy. But regardless of this arrangement the mechanical engineer's office prepared a revised design which was built at Altoona, in the Juniata Shops July, 1900. Carrying road number 269, its cab was placed at the rear of the locomotive which was lengthened out giving it a longer total wheelbase. Instead of the rigid trailing truck on class E1, a two-wheel radial truck was used. This new engine was given a class E2 designation.

After a thorough checking concerning its operating performance, long a Pennsy practice, a new design was prepared based upon No. 269. Many of its details were retained, but some modifications were considered advisable. This first engine, No. 65, built in May 1901, was assigned to the West Jersey & Seashore Railroad, a new railroad title representing the combined Camden & Atlantic, and old West Jersey Railroads, which in 1896 came into Pennsy control. This engine was also given an E2 classification and the first E2, No. 269 was re-classified as an E1a. The new E2, engine 65, had a larger grate, and more tubes which increased the heating surface. Boilers on 269 and 65, both used radially stayed, or round-top firebox roof sheets. The reason for this was the fear that the Belpaire might be too heavy due to its particular constructional features.

The E1a and E2, had a new arrangement of spring equalization between the drivers on each side and the rear truck. This was accomplished by connecting short beams with a half-elliptic spring. This general chassis layout lasted for many years even after a newer design of back end spring equalization came into use on later designs of light Atlantics.

In October 1901, for the rugged grades of the Pittsburgh Division, Juniata turned out engine 621, class E3, construction number 833. Cylinders of this engine were increased from the E2's 20½ × 26 inches to 22 × 26 inches. With these larger cylinders the tractive force jumped from 23,800 lb. to 27,410 lb.

In all other respects the E3 duplicated the E2, and all those early Atlantics built up to the end of 1901 had one dome atop the boiler. In 1902 new locomotives of the Atlantic type had the sandbox separated from the steam dome, and this action was taken on other single-domed engines as years went by.

With the introduction of the Belpaire firebox on the Atlantics in 1902, and which differed considerably from the design used on class E1, the letter "a" was added to their E2 and E3 classification. On Lines West other Atlantics with Belpaire fireboxes, due to some constructional variations were classified as E2b and E2c. The former of which ten had first been built in 1903, had originally been given the E2a label, but soon had it changed to E2c.

Flat-side view of No. 269, engineer's side.

Another view of No. 269, fireman's side.

Revised design of Atlantic, but still using six-wheel tender. Engine No. 269 built at Altoona in 1900, was again the work of Axel Vogt. Cab was in the conventional location. Steam dome and sandbox were combined in one unit. This engine was originally known as class E2, but a later version was developed, and No. 269 became class E1a, when the new E2 class made its appearance.

Final design of the single-domed E2 class engines. Engine 1968, though not the first of this group, was built in 1901 at Juniata Shops and set the pattern for the Atlantics that followed. While customary to refer to these engines as "light Atlantics" they were not so considered at the time of their construction, for by the standards of that time they were really big engines. It was only when comparing them with the mighty E6s class Atlantics of the Pennsy that this differentiation was made between "light" and "heavy" Atlantics. Engine 1968 was in a bad wreck at Paoli in 1906, and once gave Prince Henry of Prussia, the German Kaiser's brother, a ride in her cab. Four-wheel pedestal type trucks designed by the Pennsy, with an increase in tank capacity replaced the rigid six-wheel tenders with beneficial results. Note the absence of the outside bridge pipe from the dome to the cab turret, and side feed injector check valves. From then on the Atlantics had these valves placed on the backhead of the firebox.

This picture illustrates the clean-cut lines of the single dome E2 class locomotives. The poise and grace of a "high-stepping trotter" are exemplified by engine No. 1435 as it heads west with train No. 5, the Pennsylvania Limited, through West Philadelphia in 1901. This was one of the most colorful trains to ever grace the rails in the United States. Under the belt rail beneath the window sills, the cars were painted green, above the coloring was cream white, and the letterboard was tuscan red with gold leaf lettering and striping. All cars were owned and operated by the Pullman Company, including the dining car. Around 1904 the color scheme of the cars again became tuscan red, though still Pullmans. The dining car continued to be operated by Pullman and was so indicated on the letterboard until 1909.

   Chart showing record of run made by single-domed E2 class engine No. 1986, built in 1901, with a nine car train.

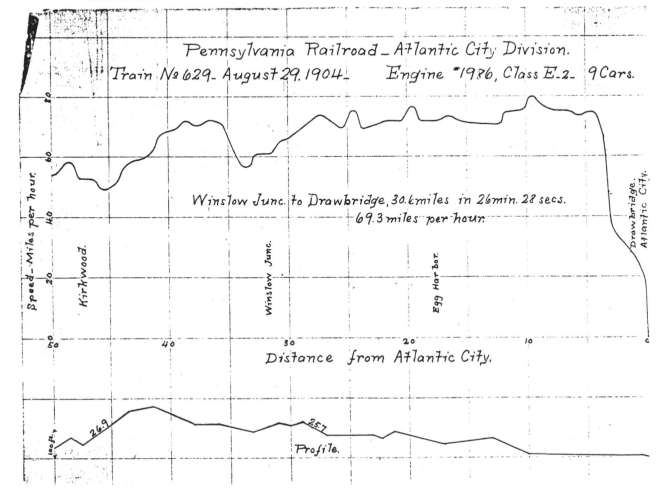

Pennsylvania Railroad — Atlantic City Division.
Train № 629 — August 29, 1904 — Engine #1986, Class E-2 — 9 Cars.

Winslow Junc. to Drawbridge, 30.6 miles in 26 min. 28 secs.
69.3 miles per hour.

Speed — Miles per hour.

Kirkwood.

Winslow Junc.

Egg Harbor.

Drawbridge. Atlantic City.

Distance from Atlantic City.

Profile.

Taken in 1902 on the Main Line between Philadelphia and Harrisburg. An E2 Atlantic takes the "Fast Mail" train No. 25, westbound.

Engine 1435 which headed train No. 5, over the Philadelphia Division when the gaudy colored Pennsylvania Limited was known to Pennsy men as the "Yellow Kid" a cartoon character of the time. Tender still carried plain P. R. R. on its sides, but shortly after the single word PENNSYLVANIA appeared on the tank sides of all new and many old engines operating east of Pittsburgh. Lettering was in gold leaf, as usual. Engine 1435 was built at Juniata in 1901.

A trim looking E2 class Atlantic with the sandbox separated from the steam dome. This was a neat job with even the sand pipes located under the boiler jacket. Martin Lee had engine 2034 several times and commented "This engine is fine."

A class E2 engine heads west with a consist of old non-vestibule head-end rolling stock. Train is passing through West Philadelphia and time was 1901. Old "K" interlocking tower can be seen in the background.

There was a tragedy associated with this picture. Paul T. Warner, a great locomotive historian, and photographer of this scene told me that this train, No. 21, then known as the Chicago-St. Louis Express, had just killed a man as he tried to beat the train at a grade crossing in his horse and buggy just east of this spot. The heavy train had stopped and then started with engines and both firemen working hard. The first engine No. 1979, was a single-domed E2 built in 1902, and the second engine was a D16a class locomotive. Bracket post signal No. A-46 typical of most signals on what was then the Philadelphia Division, puts the location just west of Devon station. Brightly painted semaphore blades are giving the two westbound tracks clear signals. Paul Warner recalled how the elderly gray-haired engineer on No. 1979 sadly shook his head as the engine passed him.

A class E2b engine speeding a westbound Fast Mail for Chicago on the Fort Wayne Route. Train is approaching Columbia City, Indiana.

The Manhattan Limited bound for Jersey City terminal and New York, passing the Philadelphia Zoo located at the left of the picture.

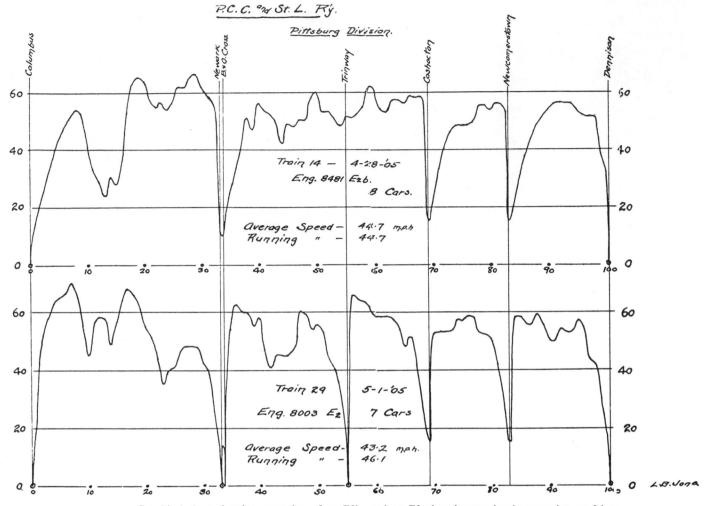

Graphical chart showing operation of an E2b, and an E2 class locomotive in operation on Lines West between Columbus and Dennison, Ohio. These runs took place on the Panhandle southwest route which branched off to the left west of Pittsburgh, Pa. This chart was made by Lloyd B. Jones, who later became Engineer of Tests of the Pennsylvania Railroad at Altoona.

This is a record of the car consist and engine numbers involved in the preceding chart. Train No. 14 was a New York bound express from Indianapolis. It became train No. 6 east of Pittsburgh. Train No. 29 was "The St. Louis Special" which ran west on the Panhandle line from Pittsburgh.

Train 14

		Due
Lv Columbus	12-50-25	12-50
Arr Dennison	3-4-48	3-14

Elapsed time — 2-14-23
Running time — 2-14-23

3 mail
1 combination
1 coach
1 diner
2 Pullmans

Eng 8481 - E2b Schenectady 5-03

Train 29.

		Due
Lv Dennison	4-29-45	4-30
Arr Trinway	5-27-35	
Lv "	5-29-30	5-30
Arr B&O. Cross.	5-58-5	
Lv " "	6-0-30	
Arr Newark	6-2-20	
Lv "	6-6-55	6-3
Arr Columbus	6-48-52	6-50

Elapsed time — 2-19-7
Time in stops — 8-55
Running time — 2-10-12

3 Adams Express
1 Combination
1 Coach
1 Diner
1 Pullman

Eng 8003 - E2 Juniata '02.

36

Lines West engine No. 7482, class E2b, built at Juniata in 1906. After being equipped for superheating some years later it became class E7s.

This Lines West Atlantic No. 7315 was built at Juniata in 1902, and originally given an E2a classification. It was generally similar to the E2a Atlantics operating east of Pittsburgh, but differed in having cylinders cast in two parts right and left, with half a saddle each bolted together at the centerline. This was unlike eastern Atlantics where the two cylinders and saddle were of three part construction. Later this split-saddle design using slide valve cylinders became class E2c. Atlantics with "inboard" piston valves like those New York Central Atlantics were first also known as class E2a, but later became class E2b. On Lines West light Atlantics cylinders were in direct alignment with the stack centerline instead of having the stack protrude 5¼ inches ahead of the cylinder centerline.

Engine 744, class E3a built Juniata 1904, heads train No. 1, the "Fast Line" one of the oldest named trains in the United States on its westbound run. Date was 1904 and as can be seen engine 744 looks quite new. The old type and class of RPO car also dates the scene. Cars to right show a southbound train from New York, after leaving tunnel and cut from the underpass tracks which enabled trains from different directions to operate without interference with each other. This clever bit of engineering was completed in 1904. Car at extreme right is a Pennsy wooden dining car with vestibules at each end and wide windows without top transom sashes or "gothics" as used on Pullman cars at the time. Train No. 1, shortly after this photograph was made, had its name changed from Fast Line to Main Line Express.

Train No. 5, the aristocratic Pennsylvania Limited passes through West Philadelphia around 1906 on its run to Chicago. Engine No. 1586 class E3a, built at Juniata in 1903, is all shined up and as neat as a pin. Note older style long pilot, and coal boards on tender. Train was composed of normal consist of six wooden Pullman cars which could well have been named in the following order from engine:

Parlor-Baggage Car	Cassius	Sleeping Car	London
Pullman Dining Car	Lucullus	Sleeping Car	Logansport
Sleeping Car	Cresheim	Observation Comp't.	Fortuna

A westbound train at Trenton, N.J., runs through the overflowing creek that runs alongside the station far to the right. This picture gives a good close-up of the Pennsy's full-width vestibule wooden coaches. These cars rode very smoothly on their four-wheel trucks. The roof of the station building at the right looks the same today, and a bridge, but much wider still crosses the tracks with stairs to the platforms. Platforms at Trenton were then at track level, but in 1923 were raised to permit entrance into cars without climbing car steps. Both platforms were island type with tracks on both sides of the east and westbound tracks. Scene was taken in October 1903 when exceptionally high water rose to cover the tracks.

Engine No. 116, class E3a of the Philadelphia Division, and built in 1903, heads the first section of the Pennsylvania Limited as it passes through West Philadelphia, in the days when "Teddy" Roosevelt was President of the United States. Engine had just passed automatic signal No. 1, and part of the train has not yet passed under the 34th street bridge. Note smoke issuing from roof stack on Pullman Dining Car that was featured on this train up to the year 1909.

Engine 2771, class E2a built at Juniata in 1905, standing near the Meadows coaling dock in February 1912.

Train No. 25, the Fast Mail being hauled by E3a class engine 744. Bridge in background is 34th street, West Philadelphia. Tall mast signal is automatic signal No. 1, and semaphore blades have automatically gone to stop position. Year was 1904 shortly after engine had gone into service. In 1906 the name of this train was changed to "Chicago Special" and in 1913 the June timetables listed it as the "Metropolitan Express." Note what was called the "long pilot" on No. 744. In 1906 a smaller pilot was used from thenceforth on the light Atlantics built up to 1913. First car, an Adams Express Company car, has a U.S. Mail card inserted in a slot which can be seen in back of the tender. Second car was a United States Mail, Railway Post Office car where mail was worked enroute.

An E3a class engine takes a heavy wooden car train across the double-tracked Schuylkill River bridge in 1907. The old style wooden Pullmans are quite obvious.

Mail and express train hauled by E3a engine 2988, a 1905 Juniata product. Train has just crossed the Schuylkill River, and main line will shortly fan out into four or more tracks for rest of run to Newark, N.J. From there two main line tracks continued to the Hackensack drawbridge in Jersey City where multiple trackage again appeared; two tracks for freight trains and two for passenger. At Waldo Avenue, the freight tracks veered to the left ending at Harsimus Cove on the Hudson River. Passenger trains ran over a sturdy four track elevated structure directly leading to the huge Jersey City train shed, also alongside the Hudson River. Freight trains turned off the main line at Waverly jumpover bridge on track No. 1, south of Newark. This arrangement went into effect in May, 1904.

This picture won a prize for photographer John S. Powell, in a contest sponsored by the John Wanamaker store in Philadelphia in 1906. An E3a (first engine) and an E2d are heading west with train No. 25, then named the ''Chicago Special.'' Powell, however, named it after its former title ''The Fast Mail.'' Note the neat roadbed, with concrete drain culvert alongside track No. 1. Automatic signal on track 4, has gone to stop position. Signal bracket supporting two masts was known as automatic signal No. 17. First car was a horse car probably being used for mail storage, second car is a baggage and express car, next three cars are wide vestibuled coaches class PK which represented the peak of the Pennsy's coaches in the wooden car era. First coach used gas lighting as can be seen by the gas storage tank under the car body. Next two coaches used electricity for lighting, and the battery boxes are located under the center of the coaches. Axle-driven electric generators charged the batteries while train was in motion, and at a predetermined low speed and when the train stopped, the batteries took over the job. Upon starting again this action was automatically reversed. Photo was taken in 1906 as train approached Narberth station after rounding the big curve between Merion and Narbeth.

Philadelphia Division engine No. 2427 passes Narberth, Pa., with an Adams Express train sometime before 1914. Engine was one of 44 E3a class locomotives built in 1903, and carried Juniata Shops construction number 1054. Locomotive still retained ''long pilot'' but had discarded spoked front truck wheels for solid disc type.

Clearly a posed publicity shot as indicated by the "faked" oversize lettering on tender tank and cars. The two locomotives belonged to the E3a class of the Pittsburgh Division. Leading locomotive is No. 2413, and train is No. 11, a rather famous mail train that ran between New York, St. Louis, and the southwest. It appears to be passing around the Horseshoe Curve, long a landmark in Pennsy history. Picture was probably taken in 1908 when a quantity of all-steel Postal and Baggage cars went into service.

Engine No. 263, class E3a built in 1905, hauls a westbound Adams Express train past Narberth, Pa., on track No. 4. It had just passed a freight train on track No. 3, which can be seen in the background. First car is a class BD of 1898 used by the Adams Express Company for baggage and express. Second car is a horse car used for the transportation of horses and grated ventilators on side indicate this.

Chapter 3
The Pennsylvania Special and a Cab Ride

On Sunday June 11, 1905, the "Pennsylvania Special" was reinstated on the Pennsy and scheduled to run the 911 rail miles (it was 912 miles from the New York Cortlandt Street ferry terminal) in eighteen hours.

This train had been put into operation on a twenty-hour schedule just three years before, but due to an expanding freight traffic which created a devastating blockage at Pittsburgh, caused the Pennsy to discontinue this train on February 1, 1904.

In the three year period between June 1902, and June 1905, the Pennsy had made several changes in extensive freight traffic cut-off routes, and stations in the Pittsburgh area, thereby, greatly easing the pressure which had retarded speedy passenger train operation. Now the prospect of an 18-hour train keeping to such a schedule regularly appeared practicable.

So here stood this fine train in the Jersey City train shed from where all top-name Pennsy trains to and from the south and west began and terminated their rail journey. To get to New York City (Manhattan Island) and Brooklyn, the finest ferryboats that sailed the Hudson River were available to this road's patrons. In 1905, all were double-decked and the larger and more powerful boats had two smokestacks which carried the distinctive red keystone insignia of the Pennsy on the stack sides. It was customary for such boats to use names of cities served by the railroad and here the lordly Pennsylvania with justifiable pride had their boats carrying far off place names like, St. Louis, Pittsburgh, Chicago, Cincinnati, and Washington. All big cities to which their trains ran, as compared to many boats of other smaller railroads which just carried names of nearby suburban communities.

Up at the head-end, engine No. 1416, class E2a, built at Juniata Shops in 1902, with engineer John Warren and Fireman, William O. Hoffman, was coupled to four cars of Pennsy standard tuscan red. Some of these named cars had been part of the Pennsylvania Limited. In following order from the engine were these cars, Cassius, Pennsy Dining Car, Narcissus, and Fortuna.

In order to help readers appreciate the "gracious living" concept available to rail travelers in those days, a description of the individual cars of this train follows:

The first car "Cassius" was a combination baggage and Pullman smoker, fitted up with costly tapestries and provided with large comfortable leather chairs. A Pullman porter was there to respond to every request. The front end of this car carried in the baggage compartment, a 15-kilowatt steam turbine directly connected to an electric generator for train lighting. The turbine was supplied with steam from the locomotive at a pressure of 80 lb. per square inch, and the direct-connected generator supplied current for the whole train. In addition each car had a Willard storage battery of 32 cells and a capacity of 280 ampere hours.

The second car was a standard dining car class Dhb of the Pennsy. Its interior resembled a private dining room of a first-class hotel. The tables were elegantly furnished with fine linen and beautiful silver. Elaborate dinners and substantial breakfasts were at the command of the train's passengers.

With engineer Warren at his post, and fireman Bill Hoffman in the gangway, engine No. 1416 backs the Pennsylvania Special to the Jersey City trainshed from Waldo Avenue passenger car yard, for the first westbound run on an 18-hour schedule between New York and Chicago. Engine 1416, class E2a, built in 1902 has old style long pilot, and sandpipes under the boiler jacket; a cleanlined looking engine. In the writer's opinion the Pennsy light Atlantics were the best looking engines of their type in this country, thanks to Theodore N. Ely, with his artistic flair, and Axel Vogt, who wrought locomotive details into efficient, yet graceful form.

The car "Narcissus" which originally formed part of the "flower fleet" of Pullmans used on the Pennsylvania Limited, had 12-sections, with one drawing room and one stateroom of latest design. Relieved of the former fancy grill work, the car was beautiful in its simplicity. Tapestries were in exquisite taste, and a maid and porter looked after the comforts of the car's passengers.

At the rear of the four-car Special was a 6-compartment, Pullman observation car "Fortuna." This car was considered the finest ever built by Pullman. The compartments were daintily furnished rooms affording complete privacy. Each one of the compartments was furnished in different colored and highest grade wood with furnishings to correspond. These woods were Circassian walnut, Tobasco mahogany, English oak, rosewood, St. Jago mahogany, and one in vermillion. In the observation part of the car many comfortable seats were provided and a stenographer with his typewriter accompanied each section of the train, and his services were free to all. One enthusiastic newspaper correspondent wrote with fulsome prose that "The train is a palace on wheels."

The foregoing relates to the first westbound run of the reinstated Pennsylvania Special, but shortly after in the summer of 1905, a reporter for the former New York Herald, named Hamilton Peltz rode various steam locomotives hauling the Pennsylvania Special from Jersey City to Chicago, 911 miles. On the occasion of Mr. Peltz's trip, engine No. 1416, again headed this speedy and luxurious train out of Jersey City. It was the assigned New York Division engine for this run and was the Division's pride. It always appeared shined up with an exhibition finish, and with polished bell, whistle and dome safety valves made a sight worth seeing.

Through the kindness of Frank Moore, a great admirer of the sterling qualities of the steam locomotive, the author is enabled to present the authentic record of Mr. Peltz when riding this train for such a lengthy distance without a break. I do not believe that a similar trip had ever been made on the Pennsy prior to that made by Peltz. Now get aboard and climb into the cab as he relates his experiences in the cabs of the light Pennsy Atlantics while heading the road's first top-name and fastest passenger train for a very long distance.

A Night on the Locomotive
of
"The Pennsylvania Special"

By Hamilton Peltz

"From New York to Chicago in eighteen hours with the man behind the throttle!

Perhaps you have made that marvelous run on the Pennsylvania Special, pampered by all the luxuries of the electrically lighted library-smoking, dining, sleeping, and compartment-observation cars, with their bathrooms and barbers, their stenographers and stock bulletins, their state rooms, easy chairs, polite porters and waiting maids, and everything else possible to coddle you and ease your journey. For a month now all that has been a common experience, and the hustling, driving business man of New York or Chicago already regards his eighteen-hour train as a matter of course, much as he does his morning paper or his after-dinner coffee.

He has forgotten, if he ever knew it, that less than thirty years ago thirty-six hours to Chicago was thought a wonderful run, and that when the "Pennsylvania Limited" cut the schedule down to twenty-three hours it was thought that even twentieth century enterprise could do no better.

But as you ate your lobster à la Newburg in the dining car or idly watched the smoke wreathing from your perfecto in the library-smoking car how many of you have ever stopped to think: How fares it with the man up in front, in the leaping, quivering cab of the locomotive, the man whose eyes must be ever riveted ahead, whose steady grip clutches the throttle—the man who holds your very life in the hollow of his hand?

Oh! it is a very different story up there amid the oil and soot, in the reeking swelter of the boiler and the scorching breath of the firebox! And that is the story which a reporter for the *Herald* was detailed to tell.

Equipped With Faith.

His special equipment consisted of an unlimited stock of faith in the man behind the throttle, a cheap suit of blue and white pin-stripe overalls, a pair of automobile goggles, a small package of rations, and a permit signed by W. W. Atterbury, General Manager, instructing conductors and engine drivers to extend to the novice the hospitalities of the locomotive cab.

It was a Saturday afternoon and in mid-summer. The great train shed of the Pennsylvania in Jersey City was as busy as an anthill. The exodus of the holiday seekers was on in earnest. They were storming the gates to take the seashore expresses for Long Branch and Atlantic City. Terminal facilities were taxed to the utmost, but no rush of holiday makers, no combination of circumstances is permitted to interfere with the prompt departure of the Pennsylvania Special. "No. 29," as she is known in the official parlance of the road, is the pet of the system and to her all else must yield precedence.

She is scheduled to pull out of the Jersey City train shed at fourteen minutes past four every afternoon, and you might safely set your chronometer from the moment Traphagen opens the throttle of his big pet and locomotive No. 1416, with an admonitory snort glides smoothly out into the sunshine from under the smoke-begrimed arch.

C. H. Traphagen, a veteran of the road, though one yet in the prime of his manhood, sat in the engine driver's box. Firing for him was W. S. Denniston, a bright-eyed, handsome young chap, whose ruddy cheeks looked as though the golf links might have tinted them rather than the scorching blast of a furnace. William Messer was the train conductor over the run from Jersey City to Harrisburg, Horace G. Clark the Pullman car conductor through to Chicago, and W. S. Richards the baggage master as far as Pittsburgh.

Engine No. 1416 backed in from the yard at four o'clock and with hardly a perceptible jolt coupled on to her charge, consisting of the combination baggage, library, and smoking car Cassius, which also carries the barber shop, the sleeping car Marigold, the dining car, and, last of the quartet, the state-room observation car Veritas. There was barely time for the conductor to introduce the novice and for Traphagen and Denniston to install him at the fireman's window of the cab when the last piece of baggage was pitched aboard, the iron gateway down at the riverward end of the train shed clanged shut, a blue-clad arm waved impatiently with a cry "All right!" and then a toy whistle blew somewhere up in the labyrinth of tubes and levers of the cab.

"Now, sit tight and look sharp; we're off," said Traphagen. Deftly as an artist fingering his brush he reached for the big steel throttle and opened it gently. Responding to his touch, the ponderous machine glided forward with a series of guttural coughs, as if impatient to be off, and as she ran out into the sunlight the chronometer hanging by the steam gauge marked exactly 4.14.

Denniston was busy hurling great chunks of fuel into the blazing maw of the firebox, which to the novice seemed witheringly hot enough already to shrivel the skin on his face. Leaning far out from the cab on the fireman's side, as much to escape the awful heat as to note our progress, the reporter watched 1416 as she threaded her way like a sentient creature through the bewildering maze of switches that criss-cross the terminal yard. Traphagen had been gradually opening the throttle. With her light train it does not take 1416 long to get under way. She has begun her race with time and every instant is precious.

Already she is rattling along at a good round pace, dodging here to one side of a locomotive and there a long line of standing cars. The fireman is tugging the bellrope now, but the ding-dong of the swinging bell comes back to the cab with a muffled and faraway sound. It is almost drowned out by the more insistent din of seething steam and the titanic pounding of giant driving wheels on frogs and rails.

Of course, those switches are all set right. It is the highest duty of every man on the line to look out for "Twenty-nine," the pet of the road. But the novice riding for the first time this hundred-and-ten-ton steed, feels first a sense of strange elation and then comes the momentary thought unbidden: She is a knowing mastodon, is old 1416, but suppose she should fall a-napping and miss her cue at one of those switches some day!

He "Let Her Out" a Little.

We are out of the tangle of rails now. Straight as a ruler across the salt meadows stretches the four-track avenue of steel. Traphagen makes a trumpet of his hands and bawls across the cab, "We let her out a little here." Back comes the injection lever and for a moment the churning of water into the pipe coils of the boiler mingles its sound with the infernal din of clanging metal and sizzling steam. Back comes the throttle another inch or two and 1416, feeling the loosened rein, begins to show her paces.

Trepidation is lost in a sense of pure exhilaration. What though the right side of the body and the right leg from thigh to instep be parboiled against the awful heat of the firebox. A tornado with a touch in it of salt ozone is rushing past the face and in at the cab window. A dozen times you clap your hand to your cap to see if it is still there. It is pulled down hard over the head, but you cannot feel it. You only feel the hair beneath it ruffling in the cooling blast. The trickling rivulets of perspiration that have been coursing down the face through its mask of coal dust and grime are dried up or dashed away in the blast.

You have caught the spirit of the race now. You long to see Traphagen give her her head. You lean far out and glue both eyes on the vista of steel ribbons stretching away to Newark. From the waist up the body is in a cyclone. From the waist down it is in a Russian bath. Perspiration is soaking through the pin-stripe overalls and trickling down into the shoe tops, but the brain is tingling with the zest of the chase and the face with the breath of the hurricane.

"She's doing quite a bit now," bellowed Denniston as he paused from tossing fuel into the dragon's mouth and swung himself up on the box to shout in the ear of the novice. It was fast work, to be sure, but by this time the ills of the flesh were forgotten and the spirit cried out, "Faster! faster!"

Newark, at first a mere blur of smoke-obscured mirage, loomed big ahead. In a twinkling it lay at our feet, and then we were dashing over the stone causeways spanning its streets. Traphagen let down the speed a notch and glanced at the chronometer.

"Nine miles in nine minutes," he said. The Pennsylvania Special had crossed the meadows at a mile a minute gait, but she was to do better—much better—than that further on. Elizabeth, Rahway, Metuchen flashed by with hardly time enough for the eye to read the names on the station signboards, and then 1416 sprang across the Raritan and through New Brunswick at speed almost undiminished.

Ever and anon a gang of track workers could be seen half a mile ahead on some straight stretch of roadbed, tinkering at the stone ballast. Reaching for his whistle cord, Traphagen let out a succession of long warning shrieks, and barely time there was for the toilers to look up, seize their tools, and scurry to cover when 1416 dashed past them and left them mere dots behind.

At Monmouth Junction for the first time 1416 "scooped" water. This hundred-and-ten-ton monster of the "Atlantic" type, which had been devouring fuel at an astounding rate all the way from Jersey City, was thirsty now. She had to have a drink to replenish her depleted tanks, but the Pennsylvania Special's fast schedule from New York to Pittsburgh contemplates no such obsolete crudity as a stop to take water, so 1416 simply scoops it as she runs.

All the way out from Jersey City, as each of the distance and home signals of the block system sprang successively into view, the voice of Traphagen or of Denniston, or often as not, both simultaneously, could be heard bawling out some strange and to the untaught ear incoherent ejaculation. To the novice there seemed at first something ominous and menacing in the sudden shout of an expletive that sounded to him like "Hi!" with a sharp falling inflection. He wondered for a time if one or both of these watchful men had not sighted peril ahead or at least a cow on the track. But presently he learned that what they cried was "White!" The rules of the road, for extra precaution, require that both engine driver and firemen shall call the signals to one another. So long as the cry is "White!" and not "Red!" it means that all is well. It is the tower signal man's voucher of a clear track ahead.

So the cry of "White!" or, as Denniston after modified it, "White eye!" had grown monotonous to the novice and it now fell upon his ears dully. But suddenly here, near Princeton Junction, comes the cry from both about at the same instant, "Red!" It was not the cry of excitement, but was uttered in such cool, deliberate tones that for a moment the writer, who had seen nothing amiss, thought his ears had deceived him. But a glance at Traphagen showed him already quietly at work with his levers. First he had gently touched the air-brake controller, a brass-handled switch not unlike the motorman's controller on a trolley car. The strident hiss of compressed air was heard above the roar and then the master toyed with his speed lever.

Instantly the unbridled speed was checked. Another touch of the air controller brought it a little further around its arc and again the speed slackened, but so gradually that no shock was felt. Except in cases of extreme emergency no skilled engine driver puts his brakes on hard and fast at a single impulse. To do so would make havoc in every car behind him, turning chairs, tables, and probably passengers topsy-turvy. It is a point of pride with your expert to slow down and stop his mile-a-minute flyer so gently as not to spill the water or the coffee from glasses and cups in the dining car.

So Traphagen deftly coaxed his charge to a standstill until the brakes set hard and fast. A distance signal had been set against him by an alert tower man, who thought he saw a curl of smoke from a "hot box" as the train swept past his station. Out tumbled the curious passengers to see what was the matter and down jumped Traphagen with a ready bucket of water. The trouble was trifling, but it sufficed to put No. 29 nearly four minutes behind her schedule at Princeton Junction, and that was serious enough. It is hard to make up lost time on a schedule so swift as this, but the novice rejoiced secretly when Denniston nudged him as we got into motion again and whispered:—

"Now 'Trap' will let her out. We'll go into Philadelphia on time yet. We lost eight minutes not far from here the other day, but he took her into Harrisburg on the dot. That was the day we ran 189 miles in 202 minutes and made parts of the run at a gait of seventy-five miles an hour."

48

Settled Down to Business.

"Trap" had quit fuming now and from the way he pulled things open he evidently knew what was expected of him. He made no promises, but glanced at his watch and settled down to business. He drove his engine across Trenton with a long-drawn whoop of the whistle and dashed over the Delaware and into Pennsylvania at Morrisville at so lively a pace that, if you had not known it of old, you could hardly have read the signboard at midstream on the bridge which marks the State line between New Jersey and Pennsylvania.

Bristol and Andalusia flew by. At Torresdale the towering derricks of Philadelphia's new filtration plant were momentary features of a kaleidoscopic landscape. Tacony and the big mills of Fitler's, Bridesburg, and Frankford vanished in turn, and then came the serried red brick and white marble rows of North Philadelphia, which is as near to the real Philadelphia, centering about the Broad Street Station, as No. 29 has time to go. In the Colonial structure which marks the North Philadelphia stop, formerly known as Germantown Junction, the air-brakes again shrieked a final hiss and the flyer came to her first scheduled halt.

Traphagen's eyes had been watching the clock and also the landmarks. He leaned back on his leather-cushioned rest with a smile and held up the face of his watch. It was just thirty-nine minutes past five o'clock. The Pennsylvania Special was a minute ahead of schedule.

"Forty-five miles in thirty-five minutes," said the engine driver. "That's not bad." The train had run from Jersey City to Philadelphia in eighty-five minutes.

Barely two minutes sufficed to stretch cramped legs with a jump from the locomotive cab to the station platform, and then No. 29 must be off again in her inexorable race with time. Those two minutes Traphagen employed pouring oil from a long-necked can into crank-shaft bearings and other mysterious places, and sundry mechanics with long hammers employed them in testing the car wheels of the whole train for possible weak spots, as they did at every stop.

Forging ahead again, the panorama changed to one of beautiful suburban estates. Smooth areas of velvety greensward marked the wealthy homes of Bryn Mawr, Wayne, and Paoli. We were now speeding over the Philadelphia Division of the Main Line, and at many points the well-kept gardens of Philadelphia's elect stretched in unbroken verdure right down to the line of the steel highway. In one of them a lithe-limbed greyhound essayed a race with the Pennsylvania Special. Fleet as the creature was, we passed him as though he were a china dog cast in the pose of the chase, and his defiant yelp was lost in the rushing whirlwind behind us.

Approaching Harrisburg, the men from the steel mills ranged along the tracks shouted a greeting, which Traphagen good-naturedly acknowledged with a "toot! toot!" from his whistle. Lights were twinkling from the windows of the houses as we ran into the Pennsylvania State capital, but there was enough of twilight left to display the lofty dome of the new Capitol Building dominating the picture. Directly in the path of the train the myriad switch lights of the railroad yard flashed like an army of fireflies. Threading her way through them all, 1416 pulled up at the Harrisburg station a trifle ahead of time, at thirty-five minutes past seven o'clock.

Her work was done there and so was Traphagen's. Both now were due for a well-earned rest. It was interesting to note how this iron-nerved man relaxed now that his task was done. He dropped the throttle almost with a sigh of relief, and when his guest turned to thank him he had words of praise only for his engine. "Isn't she a beauty?" he said. "Glad you enjoyed the run. There isn't a better engine in the country." Every engine driver with whom the writer traveled said the same thing of his own pet.

In less than five minutes 1416 had pulled out for her night berth in the roundhouse and 2015 had backed down and coupled on for the night run over the Middle, or Mountain, Division. R. H. Greenwood was the engine driver of this locomotive, with C. Farmington as his fireman. M. H. Melvin succeeded to the post of train conductor. From this point a fourth occupant of the cab was Charles Douglass, traveling engineer of the division, who is making the trip from Harrisburg to Altoona almost daily on the fast trains to note points where curve elevations may be improved on this most arduous division of the whole run to Chicago.

At Harrisburg the novice, feeling hungry, found that the package of ham sandwiches, which had lain at his feet, close to the firebox, had suffered. The ham was almost broiled and the bread was toasted, while a bag of peaches were in a state of sizzling stew. A waiter from the dining car was welcomed when he thrust into the cab a plate of broiled chicken and vegetables neatly tied up in a napkin, with the compliments of the steward.

A Night Climb.

And now began the most weird chapter of the journey, a night climb up the Allegheny Mountains through squalls of rain that stung the face like sleet, a dash into the darkness with only the lights to guide aright, with the frowning silhouette of the mountain side looming on one side and the abyss often yawning on the other. Up the steep grade leaped 2015 as Greenwood pushed her to the task. There must be no shirking because of grades or darkness or abysmal depths below. The schedule is fast even in the mountain reaches.

In the cab all is dark save for the fitful glow of a small lantern illuminating the water gauge and the dials of the chronometer, steam gauge, and the steam regulator of the dynamo, which from its place, back in the combination car, is flooding the passengers with radiant light in the snug cars behind. Again and again Farmington swings open on its long iron chain the door of the firebox to toss in more fuel. Then momentarily the cab is ruddy with the fiery gleam from the furnace. Mountain side and gorge are revealed in the red light like some hellish inferno through which we are plunging and the fireman is a sweltering demon. Then the door swings shut again, blotting out the picture, to leave all more darkly mysterious than before.

Douglass continues to call the signals. "A fireman on this division," he roars into his neighbor's ear, "has no time to ride the box. He has to keep stoking her all the time."

Rain is now slanting down in long, lance-like shafts. Douglass rigs back the plate glass storm window and fastens it securely with an iron hook to shield our faces from the lashing drops as we peer out ahead, cheek by jowl, through the blackness. It is only a six-inch-wide strip of iron-bound glass, set at right angles to the side of the cab and outside of it, but it partly breaks the violence of the whipping gale of wind and water. In his hand Douglass holds a wad of cotton waste, with which alternately he mops his face and then wipes clean the rain-dashed outer surface of the storm window.

To his guest Douglass had given a similar ball of cotton waste. It is the courtesy of the cab to do so. The absorbent serves conveniently alike as a hand towel, a wash rag, and a perspiration mop. When the fireman turns on his hose to flush out the grime and coal dust from behind the firebox it is pleasant to hold that bunch of cotton waste under the stream and then color it gradually, meerchaum-like, with the soot from your fevered face and hands.

Just ahead looms out of the night a triangular display of green and red lanterns. They are hung from the rear of a long train of freight and ore cars bound westward like ourselves. It looks as though we must surely douse those lights and telescope that train, but that is only a delusion. The track swerves slightly just ahead and we go careening past the lights and the loaded tons of ore close enough to reach out to them and probably to lose an arm. The novice thought that freight train was standing still until the sight of the driving wheels of its locomotive in rapid motion surprised him.

That train is moving at twenty miles an hour," yelled Douglass, "but we're doing better than sixty now. Look ahead. See the fire belching from our stack. She's doing about all she can do now on such a grade."

On this tortuous Middle Division, with the exception of one or two good stretches, there is hardly a continuous two miles of straight roadbed. The Juniata, winding its sinuous mountain course, is crossed fourteen times on stone bridges within a space of a few miles. At two such points the new masonry bridges are not yet completed. Over the old structures the mighty Pennsylvania Special has to slow down nightly to the modest pace of twenty miles an hour. As the schedule at present does not allow enough margin for these "controls," the lost time must be made up elsewhere before Altoona is reached. Four minutes were thus lost from the schedule, but on a good piece of road near Huntingdon, Greenwood almost balanced accounts by reeling off a run at the rate of seventy-seven miles an hour, and later he made his engine rock over the rails like a ship laboring in a gale, while Douglass, who held the watch on the racer, announced several miles at the rate of a mile in forty-five seconds, or 80 m.p.h.

Altoona was reached on time, at ten minutes past ten o'clock. There we dropped the dining car. The steepest climb of all lay just ahead until we reached the mountain tops at Cresson. Greenwood retired rain-soaked with 2015 and W. R. Jones, familiarly known as "Bill," one of the most genial engine drivers on the road and one of the best, backed down his own particular pet, No. 1605, for the run over the Pittsburgh Division, with J. C. Potts as fireman. J. E. Thorn here took charge as train conductor, and an extra locomotive was ranged up in front of 1605 to help pull up to the summit, where she dropped off on a Y-switch without interference or stoppage.

Rounding the Horseshoe.

Now the Special rounded the famous Horseshoe Curve, but in the black rain-scourged night the great bend and the chasm below it were lost in one impenetrable pall of gloom. Peering out the cab window, we could see our train bending like a bow as she swung around, displaying her rear lights, and it was easy enough to feel the hundred-ton machine on which we rode list over as she took the curve. The novice, in his zeal to fathom the depths, unwisely pocketed his automobile goggles and regretted it the next minute when some bituminous samples out of the stack of the pilot engine smote his eyes and cheeks like hot bird shot, and started unbidden tears coursing down soot-stained cheeks.

Beyond the summit came a wild run with loosened rein down the mountain slopes. Old 1605 took the bit in her teeth as she galloped down through the fateful Conemaugh Valley and into Johnstown of tragic memory. The steel mills were aglow with vivid life, and further on, near Greensburg, long rows of flaring coke ovens made the trackside luminous with serried fires, like the bivouac of an army. Jeannette, Braddock, the scenes of historic industrial struggles, were flaunting their beacons to the sky. Next the straggling expanse of the East Liberty Stockyards, then another fairyland of glistening switch lights, spanned by steel bridges, showing the block signals, and flanked by brilliantly lighted signal towers, and then the hissing of the air brakes as No. 29 pulled into the Union Station at Pittsburgh. She was on time, as usual. It was half an hour after midnight by Eastern time and an hour earlier by Central time.

After a five-minute stop and another change of engine and crew, the Special was off for her run across the more level stretches of Ohio and Indiana. Twice again she changed horses in the long relay race across four great States, once at Crestline, Ohio, and again, for the final sprint, at Fort Wayne, Ind.

Tired nature revolted. Rocked in the swaying cab to a titanic lullaby of infernal sounds, the novice drowsed off into a fitful sleep, from which ever and anon he roused with a start, only to hear the hackneyed but reassuring cry "White light!" and to relapse into a contented state of semi-consciousness.

As 29 rolled into Englewood early in the morning the suburban Chicago girls were on their way to early church and the peal of church chimes mingled not unmusically with the clanging bell of the locomotive. On the tick of schedule time, at five minutes of nine o'clock, the Pennsylvania Special discharged her passengers in the Chicago station. A tired, muscle-sore, black-faced novice, as swarthy of feature now as any of the Pullman car porters, shed his soot-stained overalls in the baggage car. He then sought a life saving station, where a good Samaritan extracted bituminous coal specimens from under one eyelid and afterward administered a delectable Turkish bath, a shampoo, and a facial massage.

The Pennsylvania Special east bound is known as "No. 28." When she left Chicago that afternoon at a quarter to three o'clock she carried as one of her pampered passengers a man normally clothed and in his sound mind, resolved, despite inflamed eyes, upon enjoying all the ease of luxurious travel.

Yet he had to confess as he crossed the Hudson for the second time within forty-two hours, that the run with 29 was more interesting than the trip on 28."

END

But despite the fact that the Pennsylvania Special matched the New York Central's "Twentieth Century Limited" in every way, the Century until the end of its days got the lion's share of the New York-Chicago traffic. For this the genius of George Daniels, that energetic, outgoing salesman of the Central's passenger service was primarily responsible. For in naming the train itself, he established it in the public's mind as a leader of all that was newest and best in railroading for the present century.

Still, I personally liked the word "Special" for in railroading lingo, (about which, I fear, the general public cared little) it implied a train with running rights over everything on the road; it meant something distinctive, set apart from others, and on the Pennsy it meant their very best—the Pennsylvania Special!

There was, however, a Pennsylvania Limited, another train that left much earlier in the day. With both trains running between New York and Chicago, as Limiteds on an extra fare basis, and solid Pullman equipment, (no coaches) irritating and undesirable confusion to travelers occurred too frequently. Pennsy management finally considered it advisable to make a name change for the Pennsylvania Special, which would make it quite unlikely to associate one train with the other. On November 24, 1912, the Pennsylvania Special was renamed "Broadway Limited" and operated on a 20-hour schedule. Heavy wartime traffic due to World War 1, caused the train to be withdrawn from service on December 1, 1917, by order of the War Board, but on May 25, 1919, the Broadway Limited was restored on its 20-hour schedule. In the following years the Broadway's schedule was consistently reduced until it covered the distance between New York and Chicago in 16-hours westbound, and only 15½-hours eastbound. This latter timing was said to be the fastest service offered between these two cities.

Then came a sad day when the Broadway was combined with "The General." No longer was it solid Pullman, and coaches became part of its consist. Even its train numbers were changed as the magic, and traditional numbers 28 and 29, were obliterated and became numbers 48 and 49 of the comparative newcomer. The Broadway Limited has become a sad and pointed reflection of the depths to which this once Premier Pride of the Pennsy has fallen.

The author can heartily recommend to anyone wishing to enjoy the thrill of taking a similar lengthy ride in the cabs of Pennsy steam locomotives operating the "Broadway Limited" in February 1931, that they read RIDING THE LIMITEDS LOCOMOTIVES, by Colonel Howard G. Hill, USAR (Ret.) This book is published by SUPERIOR PUBLISHING CO. 708 Sixth Ave. Box 1710, Seattle, Washington 98111. Col. Hill made the complete run from Penn Station, New York, to Union Station, Chicago, on this overnight trip. Much technical and statistical data is included in Col. Hill's unique experience.

The Pennsylvania Special headed by No. 1416, on its first 18-hour run as it speeds through the plush main-line suburbs west of Philadelphia. This scene shows the train just after it had passed Wayne station, Pa., on its westbound run. The photo was taken by Pennsy's official photographer, William H. Rau, of Philadelphia.

This newspaper illustration speaks for itself. No. 1416 has just pulled train 29, into North Philadelphia station where a large crowd of people viewed it. Engineer Warren can be seen alongside the fence oiling around the big E2a.

THE PHILADELPHIA INQUIRER, MONDAY MORNING, JUNE 12, 1905

Russian Pacific coast to invasion,
hat Oyama is capable of speedily
Harbin, cutting the railway and
g Vladivostok. It is also feared
he Russians will take advantage of
mistice to improve their positions
strengthen their forces. There is
ral demand that Japan should care-
ateguard its interests if an armis-
declared.
lay brought no important develop-
in the situation. No information
ning Russia's formal answer to
ent Roosevelt's proposal has been
l in Tokio, and the government
ved an attitude of silence.

Armistice Not Discussed

question of an armistice, which will
the bayonets of the two enormous
facing each other on the Man-
n frontier, has not been discussed
It is believed, however, that an
ce will be speedily concluded.
dent Roosevelt's instructions to
an Minister Griscom were delayed
usmission and did not reach the le-
until late yesterday afternoon. A
message on Thursday brought the
t intimation of prospective peace
ations, but pending the receipt of
rmal message from President Roose-
nd the transmission of Japan's re-
the censor refused to allow the
mission of press telegrams bearing on
bject.
information was withheld from the
until 6 o'clock to-night, when the
n Office issued a statement contain-
resident Roosevelt's letter and For-
Minister Komura's response, and
rs were quickly on the streets of
apital with extra editions of the
apers.
Japanese plenipotentiaries to ar-
terms of peace are already under
ion. The names of Marquis Ito,
r Kataura, Foreign Minister Ko-
Marquis Yamagata and others are
ted for possible heads of the com-

lar estimates of Japan's terms of
vary widely and include both in-
y and cession of territory. It is

THE PENNSYLVANIA SPECIAL AS IT LEFT PHILADELPHIA

Lloyd steamer Kaiser Wilhelm der
Grosse with my family. In the meantime,
I am renewing acquaintances here.
"I observe in the press the use of my
name as the probable peace envoy, but
that is wholly without my authority or
knowledge."

FOUR WERE HURT IN TROLLEY CRASH

PENNSY SPECIAL DASHES WEST AS

The eastbound Pennsylvania Special in 1905, at Englewood Station, Chicago. Engine 7373, was a class E2b, built by Alco at Schenectady, N.Y., in 1903. This class had piston valve cylinders with Stephenson valve gear, and a split, or two half saddles bolted down the centerline of the locomotive. Another class used on Lines West had split-saddle slide valve cylinders, and were originally given a class E2a designation. There was another difference between the light Atlantics used east and west of Pittsburgh. East of Pittsburgh, the centerline of the stack projected 5¼ inches in front of the longitudinal centerline of the cylinders, but on Lines West light Atlantics these two centerlines coincided. Variations such as these among others, most likely influenced the Pennsy in changing their E2a engines to class E2c. After 1903 no more slide valve cylinder E2c Atlantics were built for Lines West. Tenders on Lines West Atlantics also differed from those same type engines running east of Pittsburgh.

The original No. 7002, class E2, built at Juniata Shops in 1902. Engineer in cab is the celebrated Jerry McCarthy, who with this engine is reputed to have reached a speed of 127.1 mph when hauling the first reinstated westbound Pennsylvania Special, in June, 1905, he covered three miles in 85 seconds near Ada, Ohio.

Engine 2770, class E2a, built 1905, with five cars on the Pennsylvania Special, passes through Narberth, Pa., on its run to Chicago. The bracket signal governing track No. 3, has gone to the stop position, and has automatically protected the train from the rear.

The eastbound Pennsylvania Special has just passed Wayne station, Pa., on track No. 1 as a Paoli local rolls into the station on track 4. On track 3 a freight train hauled by an H6 sub-class engine appears in this scene in 1908.

Another all-steel section of the Pennsylvania Special in 1911. Train is running eastbound to New York, and crossing bridge No. 69, that spanned the Schuylkill River in Philadelphia. Engine is No. 3349 of the K2 class built in 1911. Dining car is the original D70 class with vestibules at each end of the car. This was the class first infiltrated into the wooden car train consists. Picture also gives a good view of the bridge's construction, and its steel span truss which was of the Pratt type, and weighed 660 tons. It was installed and put into use in October 1897, and was of the deck type. Bridge 69 was built by the Edge Moore Bridge Works, of Edge Moore, Delaware.

On this day another E2a, No. 2771 built in 1905 at Juniata, heads train No. 29, the Pennsylvania Special westbound out of North Philadelphia. The engineer is sanding the rail, for this station is on an ascending grade westbound in order to clear the Reading tracks under the fence to the left. After getting over the hump at the Reading crossover bridge, the grade descends, in favor of westbound trains.

I had to get in a picture of one of my old favorite electric locomotives class DD1. Motor No. 20, with a westbound train in 1911, approaching Manhattan Transfer at high speed. Out of the tunnels these trains both east and westbound had to make good time on the "high line" as speed restrictions at the Hackensack River draw bridge and the required five minutes to cover three miles in the Hudson River tunnels allowed for no dawdling once on the open road. Also, the maximum speed of 18 mph in Penn Station yard west of Seventh Avenue, was a factor to be reckoned with. To make their 14 minute schedule from Penn Station to Manhattan Transfer, start to stop, regardless of train weight, meant that the old DD1's had to roll—and fast! In later years the Broadway Limited was only allowed 12 minutes for the 9 miles run. With speed restrictions for nearly half the distance "they sure had to step on it" as one engineer put it. Direct current at 650 volts was delivered to shoes on the sides of each four-wheel truck, depending upon which side the third-rail was located. A small overhead pantograph collected similar current from an overhead third-rail when operating on certain tracks in Penn Station territory. After AC displaced DC in this area the Long Island Rail Road gladly took over the DD1's and used them for years in freight and passenger service. One DD1 still exists at the Strasburg Railroad Museum where I hope it will soon go on display. Its appearance and numbering, however, have been changed from the days when DD1's ruled the high line! These DD1 electrics also had a great nostalgic appeal, for they spanned the years between such "oldies" as the Pennsylvania Special, Metropolitan Express, Western Express, Panama-Pacific Express, Pan-Handle Express and the 24-Hour St. Louis. Many years later these same DD1's handled, the Broadway, Spirit of St. Louis, The Airway Limited, The American, and The Rainbow, all grand names and trains which, sadly enough, only one of them still running; the pseudo Broadway, no longer all Pullman, and no longer carrying those magic numbers that meant the Pennsy's Premier train, Nos. 28 and 29!

A big engine heads the Pennsylvania Special out of Manhattan Transfer on the first part of its run to Chicago. Date was June 18, 1911. Engine 3348, of the K2 class built by Pennsy at Juniata in 1911, was climbing the grade and swinging around the long curve that led to Newark, N.J., just over the nearby Passaic River. The increase in size of the big Pacific over the light Atlantics is almost awesome.

Engine 3348, class K2, leaving North Philadelphia, westbound with the Pennsylvania Special in 1911. These all-steel Pullmans had sheathed sides that simulated wooden tongue and groove boards. This was done because many travelers feared electrocution in a car made of steel during a thunder and lightning storm.

Chapter 4
Experiments and Changes

One of the big changes in Pennsy locomotive practice occurred in 1905, with the application of Walschaerts valve gear in combination with piston valve cylinders.

The first multiple application of this arrangement was made on a group of ten Consolidations built by Baldwin in 1905. These engines were designated as class H6b. With the exception of valve gear and piston valves, they duplicated class H6a, which had first been built by Baldwin in May 1901. The first engines of classes H6a and H6b, bore road numbers 1890 and 2811, respectively.

Structurally the Walschaerts gear had decided advantages over the Stephenson gear which was more inaccessible, and prevented the stronger frame bracing permitted by the outside gear. Another thing, the Walschaerts gear required only one eccentric for the valve movement, and proper distribution of steam for forward and backward motion. Instead of four heavy eccentric sheaves two lighter eccentric cranks were substituted. Elimination of the heavy eccentrics using the Stephenson gear, relieved the driving axle of a large amount of dead weight.

Nevertheless, many engineers ripe with experience preferred the Stephenson gear with slide valve cylinders. For the Walschaerts gear had a "fixed" lead, while the Stephenson had a "variable" lead. This latter was a desirable feature in a high-speed locomotive.

Despite the abortive attempt of the de Glehn compound to dethrone standard Pennsy passenger power, the road again tried this method of using steam twice. Four balanced compound locomotives were purchased in 1905, and were of the Atlantic type, closely based on Pennsy's class E3a. Two were built by Baldwin, and two by Alco, with one engine from each builder assigned to the Lines East and one to the Lines West of Pittsburgh. All locomotives at that time numbered over 7,000, operated west of Pittsburgh.

The Baldwin engines departed from Pennsy practice in introducing a new system of spring equalization between the rear drivers and the trailing wheels. Replacing the short springs and beams between these two points, was a single long beam which simplified the arrangement considerably. Pennsy took the hint and new Atlantics subsequently built at Altoona followed this design until 1910, when a new form of trailing truck and equalization system for Atlantics made its appearance.

Chief disadvantages of this method of compounding were the crank axle, which was liable to failure, and the difficulty encountered in getting at the inside cylinders and their connections.

Contemporary with these compounds were four single-expansion locomotives comprising two Consolidations, class H28, and two Prairies, class J28, of the 2-6-2 type. All four like the E29, compounds were built by Alco (American Locomotive Company) at the Schenectady Plant. As with the Atlantics one of each class was used on the road east of Pittsburgh, and one on Lines West.

The following table gives the basic specifications of these eight purchased locomotives.

Class	E28	E29	H28	J28
Builder	Baldwin	Alco	Alco	Alco
Year built	1905	1905	1905	1905
Road nos.	2759-7451	2760-7452	2762-7748	2761-7453
Cylinders, in.	16 × 27 × 26	16 × 27 × 26	23 × 32	21½ × 28
Cylinders, no.	4	4	2	2
Drivers, diam. in.	80	80	63	80
Steam pressure, lb.	205	205	200	200
Grate area, sq. ft.	55.5	55.5	55.4	55.0
Heating surface, sq. ft.	2,869	2,846	3,773.6	3,881.6
Weight on drivers, lb.	127,000	123,000	198,000	166,800
Weight, total engine, lb.	204,000	199,000	221,500	234,500
Tractive force, lb.	23,500	23,500	45,679	27,520

"Big Liz" was the name given to engine 2761, class J28, Prairie which ran on the New York Division, quite frequently at the head end of train 22, the Manhattan Limited. It is quite probable that the operation of Walschaerts valve gear with piston valve cylinders, as on the H6b class Consolidations, influenced the Pennsy to use it on the Atlantics in 1906.

Between 1905 and 1908, hundreds of H6b Consolidations were built and equipped with Walschaerts gear and piston valves. Their performance was so satisfactory from a maintenance standpoint that it caused the Pennsy to apply this radial gear with piston valves to their Atlantic type locomotives. In January 1906, engine No. 2997, class E3d, was built at Altoona with this arrangement. At the same time, though following No. 2997, was engine 3005, which was also equipped in like manner, and known as class E2d. Both classes were similar to classes E3a and E2a, respectively, with the aforementioned exceptions.

Engineers who drove these lighter Atlantics when they hauled the Pennsy's best, said that the Atlantics with the "monkey" or "grasshopper" motion (as the Walschaerts gear was called) were "sluggish" in action. One engineer in referring to an E2d said it was a "slow" engine. It does seem from actual tests that this was the case when the engines used saturated steam, but after superheating—what an improvement!

In freight train operation the Walschaerts gear and piston valves seemed to be more acceptable probably due to the fact that comparative sluggishness in speed was taken for granted.

In connection with Pennsy piston valve cylinders there was a relief valve of novel design located in a metal casing on top of the steam chests. It was first used on a B6 class switcher in 1904, and its satisfactory performance prompted its use on class H6b, and Atlantics of classes E2d, and E3d. The inventor of this device was Axel S. Vogt, with whom we have become acquainted. This was just one of the many designs with which he contributed to the improvement of Pennsy steam power.

In 1906 the General Electric Co. produced a small Curtis steam turbine direct-connected to a generator for lighting the train and locomotive lights as well, such as headlight, classification marker lamps, and cab.

It was based on the "head end" system where a reciprocating type steam engine or turbine drove a generator usually located in the combination car and supplied lighting for the train only. But in this case instead of putting the turbine-generator set in a car it was placed longitudinally on the boiler top of Atlantic type locomotive No. 1606, class E3a, of the Philadelphia Division.

The rated capacity of this device was 15 kilowatts. It weighed less than one ton, being small enough to be placed on top of the locomotive boiler between sandbox and steam dome. The bell was relocated and placed on the roof sheet of the Belpaire firebox. An exhaust pipe ran from the turbine to a point in back of the stack. To give protection from the weather the turbine generator set was covered by a metal casing.

A big reason for placing it on the locomotive was the fact that it was nearer to its source of steam supply and, thereby, reduced condensation losses to a greater degree than when the equipment was placed in a car. In winter the train heating system losses caused by leaks between the coupled cars can jump up the coal consumption alarmingly. An application of this same type turbine-generator was made on a D16 sub-class engine, but in that case it was placed crosswise in front of the stack. With improved methods of car lighting, the head-end system was in general discontinued in the United States.

Years later the Pennsy equipped their steam locomotives with steam-turbine electric generators for use by the locomotive only, and placed the lighting unit and exhaust pipe on top of the smokebox in a crosswise position in front of the stack. Near the end of steam power the turbine generator again changed

Train 22, the Manhattan Limited passes "3" Tower on the right (hidden by the train) and the Philadelphia Zoo on the left in 1907. Engine is No. 2761, and lacks the usual Pennsy look for it is one of the two experimental Prairies class J28, purchased from Alco in 1905. The white capped baggage master in the second car indicates that the picture was taken between May and October when Pennsy trainmen wore summer uniforms with white caps. Note signal maintainer on top of signal just passed.

position. The headlight was placed on top of the smokebox and below it the turbine-generator rested on a shelf-like support that projected from the smokebox front. Underneath that was a platform used for facilitating inspection and maintenance.

Pennsy started experimenting with mechanical stokers in 1906 when they applied a Hayden stoker to a class H6a Consolidation. The locomotive operated on Lines West and proved as other stokers did at the time, that it was not a smoke preventer. It did indicate, however, that it could operate, after the fireman gained experience, in a manner that would produce a saving in coal consumption when compared with hand firing.

Around this time a mechanical stoker was invented by David F. Crawford, General Superintendent of Motive Power, Lines West. By 1910, Crawford stokers were operating on numerous locomotives of the Consolidation and Pacific types on the road west of Pittsburgh. These stokers were of the underfeed type and provided almost perfect and smokeless combustion. Years were to pass, however, before the Pennsy east of Pittsburgh put stokers on their locomotives in quantity. After

becoming General Manager, of the Lines West, Crawford left the Pennsy to become a top official in the Locomotive Stoker Company.

The year 1906 was of special import to the Pennsy. The country was in a floodtide of prosperity, and such conditions were making themselves felt on that railroad. Their project, then in full progress, to make a direct rail entrance into New York City, created a situation that reflected directly upon the motive power.

Wooden passenger cars were by law prohibited from operating in the Hudson or East River tunnels. This in turn resulted in an official Pennsy proclamation made in 1906, that all new passenger cars built from then on for them would be of all-steel construction, Pennsy also served notice on Pullman that their cars would also be required to meet the all-steel decree in order to operate into New York City.

In the meantime heavy passenger and freight traffic was putting a severe burden on the motive power especially in passenger service where additional cars were being added plus those of steel which by 1907-1908, were infiltrating into train consists.

The only option for the light Atlantics was double-heading or splitting trains into sections, both costly alternatives. This problem was more acute on the northwest region between Pittsburgh and Chicago, which put it up to David F. Crawford, General Superintendent of Motive Power, on Lines West.

Nearby, the Pittsburgh Works of Alco were still in business, and Crawford wisely chose to work with them in an attempt to solve the pressing motive power problem. For Altoona was swamped with work that had their drafting room and shops humming with activity. The nearness of the Works was a great help and made it possible for Mr. Crawford to personally supervise the design and consult with the builder's engineers speedily when questions arose. Saturated steam still powered most American locomotives and the obvious and speediest solution appeared to be a larger locomotive. Western and

Southern railroads had been using the Pacific, 4-6-2 type, with marked success, so Pennsy decided to give it a try. It was clear that the light Atlantics, as far as heavier top-name train haulage was concerned, were coming to the end of their days. Consequently this collaborative effort between Crawford and the Pittsburgh Works, resulted in a large Pacific type locomotive which came from the Works in April 1907. It was said to be the largest passenger locomotive in the world at the time. The huge boiler which necessitated shortening the stack, sandbox and steam dome considerably, was a foretaste of things to come on the Pennsy. Given a class K28 designation, and carrying road number 7067, it had a straight-top boiler with a radial stay, round-top firebox. Cylinders were 24 × 26 inches, drivers 80 inches, and steam pressure 205 lb. per square inch. Tractive force was 32,620 lb.

Engine No. 7453, the J28 class Prarie built by Alco for the Pennsylvania Lines (Lines West). It had Stephenson valve gear with piston valve cylinders. This engine ended its days on the Fort Wayne route in local Passenger service. Note the trailing truck which was duplicated on Pennsy engines, class K28, K2 and K3s. This detail was of Alco origin.

Engine 2761 finished its days in "snapper" service helping passenger trains climb the grade from Altoona to Gallitzin. No. 2761 is seen rounding the famed Horseshoe Curve as it returned light to Altoona.

As usual with a new design the Pennsy worked their neophyte Pacific plenty to see what it could do. It was on the road between Pittsburgh and Crestline, Ohio, with trains 403 and 8, that 7067 did most of her running. Here performance was most satisfactory proving that 7067 could not only handle present traffic with ease, but had plenty in reserve to speedily haul the heavier steel cars which by 1907-1908, were infiltrating train consists. The large boiler caused railroaders to refer to No. 7067 as "Fat Annie" but good naturedly, for the engine steamed freely, and for such large size rode smoothly.

The successful work accomplished by No. 7067, sold the Pennsy on the Pacific, but they decided to revamp the design somewhat to conform more to their standards. A Belpaire firebox replaced the round-top form, and straight line running boards with relocated air drums gave the engine neater lines. Other details of a minor nature were also changed, but the basic specifications, boiler dimensions, valve gear, and Alco trailing truck similar to that used on the J28 class Prairies were retained. The new design was worked out at the Fort Wayne drawing office, where the engine was given a K2 classification of which more anon in Chapter 7.

One of the Cole compounds built by Alco for Lines West. Tenders and cars on this part of the Pennsylvania Railroad were lettered "Pennsylvania Lines." Note how the inside high-pressure cylinders protrude in front of the outside low-pressure cylinders in order to give sufficient length to the inside main rod. Engine was built at Schenectady plant of Alco in 1905, class E29.

Class E28 built by Baldwin. This was a four-cylinder balanced compound similar to those built by Baldwin for the Santa Fe and illustrated by Santa Fe engine No. 507, in Chapter 5.

Alco's Cole compound No. 2760 built for the road east of Pittsburgh on the point of a westbound triple-header rounding the Horse Shoe Curve. Two E3a class Atlantics are giving a helping hand. Pullman cars of wooden construction date picture as being taken before 1911.

Altoona's first Atlantic with Walschaerts gear and piston valve cylinders. Engine No. 2997, class E3d, Juniata Shops construction number 1422, was built January, 1906. Engine features the "short" wooden pilot in place of the former "long" pilot. In fact, this short pilot was used exclusively on all passenger locomotives built from then on until the coming of the metal slat, or "chicken coop" design which appeared on the 1920, K4s class engines. No change was made in the tenders, of either the E2d or E3d at the time. The neat curves of the sandbox and steam dome reflected the artistic ability of Theodore N. Ely, Motive Power Chief, in Philadelphia. Mr. Ely, was not only a mechanical engineer of highest calibre, but his artistic flair was recognized by the American Institute of Architects when they made him an Honorary Member. These were the last Atlantics to be built with cinder chutes and slides—as were class E2d, which duplicated class E3d in every respect expect cylinder dimensions. As can be seen the Pennsy light Atlantics were probably the most handsome passenger locomotives in the United States, and combined cleancut lines with highly efficient operation, but it must be said that the efficiency was more apparent after superheating on classes E2d and E3d.

This picture of E3d engine 3006, built January 1906, shows how the higher location of the reverse shaft of the Walschaerts gear made it necessary to raise the height of the reach rod connection to the reverse shaft arm. This accounted for the "gooseneck" curve, and gave sufficient length of the arm to give enough leverage to actuate the reverse shaft when operated manually.

Brand new from Juniata Shops in 1906 and looking it, engine 3155, class E2d, pauses for a moment at North Philadelphia. Train is bound for Jersey City where passengers will detrain and board ferryboats which were the last word in elegance on the Hudson River. These boats then took passengers to either Cortlandt, Desbrosses, West 23rd Streets, Manhattan, or Brooklyn. Engineer could well be Frank Howard of the New York Division. Note how the lower half of the smokebox plate has the bolts spaced closer together than the bolts above the centerline. Reason for this was that when many hot cinders collected at the smokebox bottom there was a possibility that under certain conditions they gave forth a glowing heat that warped and buckled the front plate. The additional bolts at this critical zone worked well in preventing this. Nevertheless some later locomotives of classes E6s and K4s, had all the bolts more widely and symmetrically spaced around the front smokebox plate. I once saw a bad case of such warping on an E6s engine in Camden N.J. The plate was actually red hot and badly buckled and wrinkled. Note the cinder chute and its slide under the smokebox. No. 3155 had the "short" pilot which was applied to all the light Atlantics built after 1906. Some Atlantics on Lines West may have used this shorter pilot before then.

Another early E3d class engine built at Juniata in January 1906, with construction, or shop number 1424.

Engine 3004, class E3d, built at Altoona in 1906, descends the grade leading to the tunnel under the outbound track for the west. Connection with the New York Division was made near Girard Avenue, at "3" Tower (Mantua). Lower quadrant signals were typical of the period 1906. First car is a class MM, and the newest in wooden Pennsy Railway (RPO) Railway Post Office cars. Such a car was exhibited at the St. Louis Fair in 1904. One side was removed so that the public could see how mail clerks speedily handled a large volume of mail enroute over the rails. It was one of the "hits" of the Fair. Extra windows in these cars provided better lighting during the daylight hours. Train was from the south and bound for Jersey City, and New York.

This scene represents a train that gave its passengers "luxurious living on the rails." All the comforts associated with the Pennsylvania Special were available to those who rode the Pennsylvania Limited. Barber, bath, delicious freshly cooked meals of roasts and vegetables, and home-made apple pie—a Pennsy specialty—baked right in the dining car, plus that superb coffee and cream topped off the meal to perfection. This train was the aristocrat of the Pennsy. It catered to their patrons who appreciated a daylight ride through the beautiful Pennsylvania countryside, and were satisfied with a more leisurely approach to their destination. In this picture we see train No. 5, the westbound Pennsylvania Limited in 1906, headed by a new E3d Atlantic built the same year, as it passed through West Philadelphia. Second car is a Pullman Dining Car, which Company operated these cars on this train and its eastbound section Train No. 2, until 1909. At that time Pennsy replaced them with their all-steel D70 class Dining Cars, and took over operation. The six-car consist of train No. 5 was made up as follows:

        Pullman Parlor Smoking Car, New York to Chicago
        Pullman Dining Car, New York to Pittsburgh and Fort Wayne to Chicago
        Pullman Drawing Room Sleeping Car, New York to Chicago
        Pullman Drawing Room Sleeping Car, New York to Cincinnati
        Pullman Drawing Room Sleeping Car, New York to St. Louis
        Pullman Observation Compartment Car, New York to Chicago

The lower quadrant signals to the right are for eastbound trains leading to the underpass that made connection with the New York Division at "3" Tower.

A westbound train crossing Schuylkill River bridge No. 69, with a "monkey-motion" Atlantic at the head-end. Some of the cars are open platform wooden coaches while others are the full width vestibule type. Sixth car from engine is a wooden dining car, and year is 1906—or 1907. Through the arch under the engine can be seen part of the old Girard Avenue bridge.

An E3d engine heads a ten-car train across the longest stone arch railroad bridge in the United States. On the Philadelphia, Middle, and Pittsburgh Divisions, the E3 and its sub-classes did most of the passenger work. Here their additional tractive force due to larger cylinders were an advantage for the predominantly westbound gradient profile that ran from Harrisburg to Gallitzin, Pa. 12 miles west of Altoona. This bridge replaced one of steel built in 1877. The stone arch bridge was opened and ready for service early in 1902. It is still in daily use. The semaphore on the high signal mast gave engine crews of oncoming trains on the other side of the Susquehanna River plenty of chance to see it and regulate their speed accordingly.

Year was 1907, engine 3158 class E2d built in 1906, just after crossing Schuylkill River bridge. Train is Manhattan Limited, and is nearing "BX" interlocking tower where it will soon be on a four-tracked main line. As usual, a mail car is on the head end. It might not be amiss to give the public timetable consist of the cars that took passengers from Chicago to New York, as listed in the year 1907.

In 1908 nine new E3d class engines came onto the Lines East. Eight of these, Nos. 10, 186, 318, 917, 955, 1028, 1044, and 1067, were built specifically for the Jersey City-Washington, D.C., runs, and were assigned to the New York Division. Engine 955 was one of them, but in this picture it was pulling train No. 22, the Manhattan Limited. Picture was taken in Spring of 1908, as engine was just out of shops. Engine was probably being given some "break in" runs as was usual when locomotives were new and "stiff." Quite possibly engineer could be "Wes" (John Wesley) Hartman, whose skill at the throttle with new locomotives was a recognized fact.

All cars were of wooden construction. The RPO man leaning from the front door of first car was probably the "C in C" (Clerk in Charge) of the mail car. The second car was not a Pullman but a Pennsy Combination Car that was used in this train's consist in those days. The third car was a Pennsy Dining Car, with large picture windows. In fact the Combination Car and Dining Car were much alike in size and construction. The two Pullmans on the rear were wooden as the steel Pullmans came somewhat later. In fact, all-steel Pullman trains did not appear until September 1910, not long before the Pennsy entered New York City via the Hudson tunnels. One more thing about this locomotive; an interesting item made in France, and located on engine 955, was a speedometer in its cab. It was square faced, and measured 12″ × 12″ with a thickness of about 6 inches.

This view gives us a close-up of engine No. 955 of the E3d class. A total of nine of these engines was built and one, No. 6258, went to the Western New York & Pennsylvania Railway, but the others soon after their appearance on the New York Division to which they were assigned, went into the Jersey City-Washington, D.C. passenger service. All the Pennsy light Atlantics had an air of refined elegance, a poise, that set them apart from other American Atlantics of their day. From the graceful curves of the sandbox and steam dome to the tapered stack with its artistically flared rim, the hand of the artist as well as the engineer was seen. For the artistic touches much was contributed by Theodore N. Ely, while the blending of the eye-pleasing lines with functional utility was mainly the work of Axel Vogt. This picture was taken in the spring or summer of 1908, for the locomotive is obviously fresh out of Juniata where it was built in May of that year. Location is close to "3" tower opposite the Philadelphia Zoological Gardens. At "3" interlocking tower train No. 22, the Manhattan Limited used to change engines and crews. The New York Division engine and train crew have obligingly posed for their picture. Left to right we have the conductor, engineman, flagman (see the lanterns) and fireman. Through runs between Jersey City and Washington were inaugurated on Sunday August 16, 1908, so this photo was most likely taken before that date. White caps of the train crew were part of the uniform between the Middle of May and middle of October.

No. 955, like the other 1908, E3d engines departed in a few respects from the E2d and E3d classes of 1906. Note the absence of the cinder chute and slide under the smokebox. By 1908, the Pennsy had developed a self-cleaning smokebox to which end E2a engine 5266, had contributed much on the Altoona test plant. A new tender, class 55P58a was also used and had a much wider frame known as channel type. Length of tank and distance between truck centers were the same as class 55P58 used on the 1906, E2d and E3d Atlantics. Water capacity was unchanged but coal capacity was slightly increased. Spoked wheels, however, are still in evidence on forward and trailing truck.

Schedule and train consist of the Manhattan Limited in 1907.

MANHATTAN LIMITED TRAIN 22

Pennsylvania RR.—Parlor Smoking Car, Chicago to New York
Pullman Drawing Room Sleeping Car, Chicago to New York
Pullman Observation Compartment Car, Chicago to New York
Penna. RR. Dining Car, Chicago to Alliance and Harrisburg to New York

Schedule Train 22

Chicago, lve. 11:00 a.m. (Central time)
Pittsburgh, lve. 12:55 a.m. (Eastern standard time)
Altoona, lve. 4:05 a.m.
Harrisburg, lve. 7:10 a.m.
North Philadelphia, 9:41 a.m.
Newark, 11:23 a.m.
Jersey City, 11:37 a.m.
New York, Cortlandt St. 11:53 a.m.

Angle view of No. 3006, class E3d at Atlantic City in 1908. All engine trucks used spoked wheels on Atlantics built prior to 1910. Tender was similar to those used on E2 class Atlantics of 1901, and known as class 55P58, which meant as follows; 55 stood for 5500 gallons in water capacity, P, meant Passenger service (steam heat piping on tender to transmit steam from engine to cars) and 58 gave the height of the deck plate from the rail top. These tenders had Pennsy designed, pedestal trucks, narrow underframes only 7 ft. in width and measured 14-ft., 8-in. between truck centers. Coal capacity was 27,600 lb.

This picture was taken of a ½-inch scale model showing the K28 class locomotive No. 7067, built in 1907, by Alco, for the Pennsylvania Railroad, Lines West. It used to be enclosed in a glass case on the 16th floor of the 30 Church Street Building, New York. On this floor were located the New York City offices of the American Locomotive Company. The model was made by a man named Coombs. While some details vary from the prototype, the model with its straight-line running boards location of main reservoirs simulates a Pennsy K2 (less the Belpaire firebox and Pennsy cab) very closely.

Diagram and sectional elevation drawings of class K28 locomotive built by the Pittsburg Works of the American Locomotive Company in May, 1907. This engine was in its main specifications and details the forerunner of the Pennsy's K2 class, in fact a pilot model.

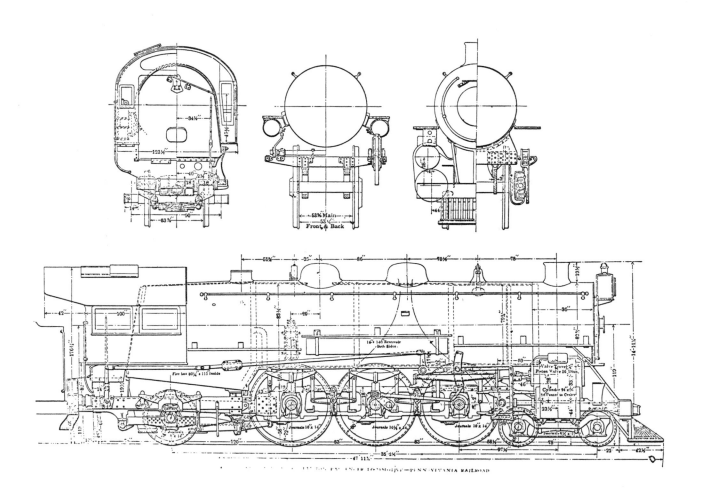

Chapter 5
Facts and Figures

In this Chapter are facts and figures concerning Pennsy locomotive operating activities not generally known. Information of historical interest during early days of the present century particularly as they pertain to the New York Division are included.

Probably the most interesting feature of this Chapter is part of the official report made by four Pennsy railroadmen who rode over 6500 miles to investigate the question of long distance runs of over 200 miles in one direction, with one engine and crew. Primary consideration was the effects such a procedure would have on the engine crew.

Another interesting part is represented by two tables which record operation of certain Atlantics in 1905 and 1908.

The first table records the lengthy distances that were made on some runs after the fireman discontinued feeding the firebox, and reclined on the seatbox. In some instances, the old Atlantics rivaled electric and diesel locomotives in easing the fireman's burden. In fact, a fireman can be more busy at times on a diesel or electric locomotive than the fireman was on these specific light Atlantics. The comparatively much smaller train heating boiler on such locomotives and more complex controls accounted for this in large part. At times they left much to be desired despite their use of the word "automatic" concerning their operation and personal attention was greatly and constantly needed.

Martin Lee, engineer on the New York Division, was a great advocate of "bank" firing. This, however, required some time-consuming preparation at the enginehouse area prior to the locomotive's departure from the "ready" track. But it did work, and the following table of runs made in 1905, was verified by Pennsy officials who rode several of these trips in the engine cab. Nevertheless, the time required to get the fire prepared militated against its use.

Advantages from this method of firing were excellent, for by "coking" the coal to a great extent, it practically produced smokeless combustion in many instances for the greater part of the trip. It also meant, with the fireman having more time to be on the lookout for signals, that two pairs of eyes were alert on the road without distraction for many miles. This was a safety feature of great importance especially in bad weather—and before the use of cab signals!

In checking these figures of the Washington-Jersey City runs, it may be somewhat surprising that the E2a showed up so well against the more powerful E3d class which had larger cylinders, and with everything else being equal, more tractive force. But from one section of the Pennsylvania Railroad Practice Book, dated April 26, 1906, this following pronouncement by Axel S. Vogt, Pennsy Mechanical Engineer, at Altoona, Pa., provides a valid explanation.

"Take, for instance, our E2a locomotive which has cylinders 20½ × 26 inches, and carries a boiler pressure of 205 pounds above atmosphere. One cylinder full of steam under that pressure weighs 2.37 pounds. Our rule is to provide 1000 square feet of heating surface for each pound weight of the steam contained in the cylinder which would, therefore, be 2,370 square feet of

Engine No. 526, class E2 built at Juniata in 1902. This is the locomotive that did such fine long distance running on small amounts of fuel between Philadelphia and Jersey City.

heating surface that should be given to this boiler; but for high-speed passenger service we increase the heating surface by 10 per cent. Strictly following this rule, the heating surface should be 2,607 square feet; the actual amount provided is 2,640. In the case of the class E3a locomotive the rule does not apply, for the reason when that class was designed it was intended for slower speeds, and it was deemed quite safe to increase the cylinder diameter from 20½ to 22 inches without expecting serious difficulty. According to the rule, the heating surface of that locomotive should be 3,003 square feet, but as a matter of fact it is the same as that in class E2a, 2,640; and where steady running on a level division is performed under high-speed conditions, like on the Western Division of the Fort Wayne Road, which is practically level, it has been found, as would be expected, that in hauling trains 28 and 29 the class E2 locomotive is superior to the class E3, for no other reason but that it can produce more steam in proportion to the cylinder volume in a given length of time.''

Wasn't the alleged (I use the word advisedly) 127 mph. speed record on the Pennsy made by a member of the E2 clan, No. 7002, class E2, with 20½ × 26 inch cylinders? But the E3 class and its sub-classes with their greater tractive force were built primarily for the Pittsburgh Division, and soon found favor on other divisions as well. In fact, some engineers were enthusiastic about class E3a. Many locomotives of this class hauled the Pennsylvania Special, trains 28 and 29, on the road east of Pittsburgh.

Pennsylvania Railroad Investigation of Long Distance Runs

For many years it had been customary to operate north and southbound trains between Jersey City and Washington, D.C., with a change of locomotives and engine crews at West Philadelphia. In earlier days this was done at Powelton Avenue Station, and later in 1903 at the newly opened West Philadelphia Station at the lower level or tunnel tracks.

A similar situation had also existed in the through passenger train service between Jersey City and Harrisburg, a distance of 194 miles. But with the construction of the New York-Pittsburgh subway tunnel in West Philadelphia in 1904, several through passenger trains between Jersey City, Pittsburgh and the west began running without engine or crew changes between Jersey City and Harrisburg, 189 miles, on December 4, 1904.

In this way only one intermediate stop was made by such trains at North Philadelphia, renamed that year from its original designation, Germantown Junction. Prior to that, through trains between Jersey City and Harrisburg, changed engines and crews at West Philadelphia, and later at Broad Street Station, when running east or west.

Many New York and Philadelphia Division men bid in on those runs because longer mileage and layovers with increased pay were heartily welcomed.

In view of the satisfactory response to the long-distance runs between Jersey City and Harrisburg with one engine and crew, enginemen on the southern trains running between Jersey City and Washing-

One of the Santa Fe's four-cylinder balanced compound Atlantics built by Baldwin in 1904. This was one of the type engines the Pennsy locomotive committee rode when investigating long-distance runs. An engine like this, No. 517, brought Death Valley Scotty's Special train into Chicago. On this run which took place in July 1905, one engine of this same class, No. 510, hit a speed of 106 mph. As you can see by the steam turbine electric-generator in front of the stack, the Santa Fe was using electric headlights long before the Pennsy.

ton, D.C., indicated a strong desire to run over two lengthy divisions, namely, the New York and Maryland, thereby emulating their brother enginemen in the east and west passenger train service.

But Pennsy officials were dubious about the practicability of a passenger train run over 200 miles—225 miles in fact, between those two cities. To make sure that the Atlantic type engines which would bear the brunt of this service could stand its severity,

a change in the former procedure was made. On June 6, 1906, through north and southbound passenger trains omitted the engine change at West Philadelphia. One locomotive was operated right through between Jersey City and Washington, but engine crews still changed at that point.

The Atlantics of the various E2, E3 class and sub-classes were able to make the run, but some difficulties arose due to the engines being "pooled"

TABLE OF DISTANCES RUN IN 1905 WITHOUT ADDING COAL
Martin Lee, Engineer on All Runs

Date	Engine	Class	Train Number	Fireman	From	To	Miles	Remarks
6/25	526	E2	63	W. H. Applegate	Tullytown, Pa.	Broad St. Phila.	27.2	None
6/28	526	E2	90	W. H. Applegate	Franklin Park, N.J.	Jersey City, N.J.	34.5	None
6/30	526	E2	63	W. H. Applegate	Trenton, N.J.	Broad St., Phila.	33.6	Had 10 cars, heavy southwest wind blowing
7/3	526	E2	63	W. H. Applegate	Princeton Jct., N.J.	Broad St., Phila.	43.3	2 minutes ahead—9 cars
7/16	526	E2	32	W. H. Applegate	Lawrence, N.J.	Jersey City, N.J.	50.2	Had 8 cars
7/21	526	E2	3rd 56	W. H. Applegate	Tullytown, Pa.	Jersey City, N.J.	62.1	Had 8 cars
8/14	2767	E2a	20	W. H. Applegate	Croydon, Pa.	Jersey City, N.J.	68.5	Had 8 cars
8/17	2767	E2a	95	M. Saxton	Monmouth Jct., N.J.	Broad St., Phila.	49.3	Had 5 cars
8/18	2767	E2a	44	W. H. Applegate	Princeton Jct., N.J.	Jersey City, N.J.	46.0	Had 9 cars— C. Downes on Engine (Ass't. Rd. For. of Engines)
8/18	2767	E2a	95	W. H. Applegate	Stelton, N.J.	Broad St., Phila.	61.4	Had 6 cars
8/23	2770	E2a	44	M. Saxton	New Brunswick, N.J.	Jersey City, N.J.	30.3	None
8/23	2770	E2a	95	M. Saxton	Princeton Jct., N.J.	Broad St., Phila.	43.3	None
8/31	2767	E2a	20	M. Saxton	Deans, N.J.	Jersey City, N.J.	37.5	None
8/31	2767	E2a	95	M. Saxton	Monmouth Jct., N.J.	Broad St., Phila.	49.3	None

TRAIN NOS. AND NAMES

63 — Southern Railway Express
90 — New York Express "Clocker"
32 — Atlantic Coast Line Express
3rd 56 — 3rd Section, C&O — Sou. Ry. Express

20 — Atlantic Express (later, Keystone Express)
95 — Adams Express, South and West
44 — Wash., Phila., and New York Express
All trains ran via Broad St. Sta., Phila., Pa.

and operated by two separate crews in each direction. This was a bit discouraging, but officials decided to stick with it and experiment further and run regularly assigned locomotives and crews the entire distance. This was done on August 16, 1908, and turned out to be a most successful operation still in use today.

But before all this came to pass, W. W. Atterbury, then General Manager, East of Pittsburgh, delegated a committee of four men in the railroad's engine service, two from the New York Division, and two from the Maryland Division, to investigate this situation on other railroads where runs of 200 miles or more each way were made and provide a report covering the results.

This committee of four railroaders covered over 6500 miles when riding the engines of several of the country's largest railroads. The information they obtained was so decisively in favor of long-distance running, backed up as it was by well presented facts and figures, that it decided the Pennsy to establish such runs as previously referred to. The official report of the Investigating Committee as presented to the Superintendents of the New York and Maryland Divisions is produced in part herewith as follows:

The President's Engine

Many years ago in the days of steam, whenever the Pennsy's President travelled he had the choice of a private or "business" car coupled to a regular train, or a Special train hauled at times by a special locomotive known as the President's engine.

Occasionally, a situation would arise where the President's engine was not at hand; then the first engine available and suitable was pressed into service. This happened with Mr. Cassatt's special run to New York in 1902, when engine 804, class D16a was called upon, and covered the 89.3 miles to Jersey City, in 79 minutes, including a slow down to 30-mph. through the streets of Newark, in order to comply with a city ordinance. But 937 hauled many top officials in a two car Special. The last car was usually known as a "set-up" or "rider" car such as were used on Adams express trains for the train crew.

During the years from the 1870's the number 937 was applied to four such locomotives that ran east of Harrisburg, Pa., as follows;

The first 937 was a 4-4-0 type with 16″ × 22″ cylinders, and 56″ drivers, and a steam pressure of 125 lb.

Following table gives a record of coal consumed on runs between Washington, D.C., and Jersey City, N.J. Eleven runs are listed from November 30, 1908 to January 29, 1909.

Record of Coal Consumption Made by Atlantic Type Locomotives
Between Washington, D.C. and Jersey City, N.J., During Special Tests

Date	Engine	Class	Train	Number of cars	Coal scoops shoveled	Pounds	From	To	Engineer	Fireman	Remarks
11/30/08	2765	E2a	56	8	182	—	West Phila.	Jersey City	M. Lee	C.S. Miller	172 scoops to East Newark, 10 scoops to J. City, "On time"
12/3/08	2765	E2a	56	8	198	—	West Phila.	Jersey City	M. Lee	C.S. Miller	"On time"
12/15/08	2765	E2a	56	Not recorded	526	—	Wash.	Jersey City	M. Lee	C.S. Miller	18 minutes late on account of Atlantic City train
12/17/08	2765	E2a	69	Not recorded	547	11,025	Jersey City	Wash.	M. Lee	C.S. Miller	"On time"
12/18/08	2765	E2a	56	6	542	11,375	Wash.	Jersey City	M. Lee	C.S. Miller	Left Washington 1-hour late, arr. J. City 50 mins. late
12/20/08	186	E3d	69	Not recorded	644	13,079	Jersey City	Wash.	M. Lee	C.S. Miller	"On time" Average 9 lb. coal per car mile
12/21/08	186	E3d	56	6	702	14,300	Wash.	Jersey City	M. Lee	C.S. Miller	Left Wash. 1 hour, 30 mins. late, arr. J. City 1 hr. 20 mins. late
12/23/08	3149	E2d	69	Not recorded	887	16,500	Jersey City	Wash.	M. Lee	C.S. Miller	Train 69, 20 mins. late
12/24/08	3149	E2d	56	5	903	16,500	Wash.	Jersey City	M. Lee	C.S. Miller	Train 56, left Wash. 1 hr. 30 mins. late, made up 10 mins.
1/27/09	3149	E2d	69	Not recorded	659	12,900	Jersey City	Wash.	M. Lee	C.S. Miller	"On time"
1/29/09	3149	E2d	56	6	700	12,300	Wash.	Jersey City	M. Lee	C.S. Miller	"On time"

Another **E2d** built in 1906, climbing the grade between Narberth and Wynnewood, Pa. Note how the offset of the piston valves outside the cylinder centerline permits the Walschaerts gear to be placed in a straight vertical line arrangement.

per square inch. On top of its pilot was a large box-like affair with large cushions of red velvet on its top and back. This was used by the officials when inspecting the road. An iron rod was also in front of them upon which they could rest their feet. The pilot was of the metal slatted type long used on Pennsy freight engines.

Second 937 was originally No. 1154, and built by Baldwin in April 1876, for the Centennial held in Philadelphia that year. After the Centennial its number was changed to 44, which it carried for years until becoming second 937. Later known as class D3 it was sold to the Strasburg Railroad and became their No. 1.

Third 937 was a class O engine numbered 558 that ran on a Paoli local for several years. When used as the President's engine it differed somewhat from the standard O class engines in external appearance. The later classification of this engine was D10a.

Fourth No. 937, was a class D16b, built at Juniata in 1906. This was the last President's engine bearing that number. An exceptional incident is associated with this engine, for it actually hauled a passenger train through the tunnels under the Hudson River, before Penn Station was officially opened to the public. It happened on Saturday, January 29, 1910, when President James McCrea, and the

Engine 3151, of class E2d, built at Juniata in 1906. Used saturated steam when first outshopped, but was later superheated and became class E3sd. Scrapped in 1938. Picture taken at Meadows.

The second No. 937. This engine was built by Baldwin at Philadelphia in 1876, and later renumbered and modified in external appearance. Originally designated as class C, it became class D3, under the new classification system introduced in 1895. It is shown at Radnor signal tower with the Philadelphia Division pay car.

Third No. 937, with Andy Chambers of the Philadelphia Division in the cab. This was a class D10a locomotive, modified somewhat from the D10a, or old class O engines as originally built.

Engineer A. B. Ryan rests his elbow on the wooden pilot beam of K2 class engine No. 997, built at Juniata in 1910. To the left stands fireman Joe McCusker, both of the New York Division. It was engineman Ryan who made the run from Philadelphia to Jersey City, 89.3 miles in 76 minutes with E2a engine 2993, built at Juniata in 1905. Date was June 16, 1912.

Pennsy Board of Directors, in a two car Special train ran over the high line from Manhattan Transfer to the new Station in New York City and return. The engineer was Andy Chambers of the Philadelphia Division, a well known veteran of the Pennsy who retired January 1, 1912.

Other locomotives east of Pittsburgh were also used by top Pennsy officials with other numberings, but No. 937 was assigned to the Pennsy's highest officers located in Broad Street Station, that inner sanctum of this once great and gigantic railroad system.

When it came to special high-speed runs, the Pennsy-east of Pittsburgh, invariably chose the four-coupled type locomotive, either American or Atlantic.

On high-speed running where exceptionally fast annihilation of distance was required, the lesser machine friction of these types as compared with the bulkier Pacific was a deciding factor. Certainly was this so as far as Theodore N. Ely, Chief of Motive Power was concerned.

A record run was made on January 23, 1911, when E2a class engine 2766, ran a two-car Special over the New York Division at an average speed of 67.4-mph. The train was made up of two cars; Pennsy business car No. 90, and one P70 as a rider coach for the train crew. One of the country's greatest financial tycoons, J. P. Morgan, was the passenger.

From its start, after changing engines at West Philadelphia, for this train had originated in Washington, D.C., No. 2766 gobbled up 70½ miles to Rahway, N.J., in 59 minutes. Motor No. 23, class DD1, took the train from Manhattan Transfer to Penn Station in 9½ minutes, just one-half minute more taken by the DD1 that hauled the Lindbergh Special in 1927. Total time from West Philadelphia to New York City 90.4 miles was 1 hour and 22½ minutes.

Another speedy run was made by engineer A.B. Ryan, between Philadelphia and Jersey City on June 16, 1912, with E2a class engine 2993, and a two-car Special. In this train were officers of the

Pennsy rushing eastward to settle a strike vote called for that day. Ryan took 76 minutes for the 89.3 miles run to the Jersey City terminal which was adjacent to the Pennsy office building alongside the trainshed. The Special train left Broad Street at 10.45 a.m., and arrived at Jersey City at 12.01 pm.

Here is a record giving dates of long distance engine and train crew runs on dates established.

Dec. 14, 1904 Passenger engine and train crews, Jersey City to Harrisburg, Pa.

May 28, 1905 Passenger train crews Jersey City to Washington, D.C.

June 6, 1906 Passenger engines run through from Jersey City to Washington, D.C.

Aug. 16, 1908 Passenger engine crews run through Jersey City to Washington, D.C.

May 1, 1909 Passenger engine crews run through from Philadelphia to Delaware Water Gap, Pa.

May 1, 1909 Baggage Masters run through Jersey City to Pittsburgh, Pa.

May 1, 1909 Freight engines and crews, Jersey City to Harrisburg, Pa.

May 1, 1909 Baggage Masters run through Washington to Boston, Mass.

Around 1907, there seemed to be an impression on certain divisions of the Pennsy, particularly east of Pittsburgh, that the wide grate was too large on some of their passenger locomotives for best results, and extensive use was made of a method of blocking off or covering part of the grate surface, usually at the forward end. The locomotives generally affected were of the E2 and E3 class and their sub-classes. The assertions in regard to this or any other method of grate area reduction were debatable. On long passenger runs it was claimed that the grate thus reduced in area was easier to fire because of its being smaller, and the active part near to the fire door coal did not have to be thrown so far to cover it.

The standard grate for the E2a class locomotive had a grate area of 55.5 square feet, as did all the light Atlantics from classes E2 to E7sa. In this numerical classification it should be pointed out that no E4 class engines were ever built, and that class E6s was a "heavy" Atlantic. There were two drop gates which were fixed, but had holes for the admission of air. The active or shaking portion of the grate had an area of about 31 square feet. Following table gives a comparison of grates tested.

This engine is similar to engine 937, the fourth, and last of the Presidents engines used east of Pittsburgh. Nevertheless, the locomotive illustrated had the distinction of pulling President William McKinley's funeral train in both directions between Baltimore, Md., and Harrisburg, Pa. This locomotive like the final 937 was a class D16b, built at Altoona Shops in 1901, as No. 3119, and renumbered 4119 in 1903. It was later superheated and operated as a class D16sb, for many years on the Northern Central Railway Company. Picture shows locomotive at Baltimore, Md.

A typical single-domed D16b, hauling what obviously appears to be a Special train. The first car is a Pullman, and the last a wooden PK class coach used as a rider, or set-up car. Train is crossing the Schuylkill River in Philadelphia, and approaching the Natural Bridge that spans the East River Drive in Fairmount Park. The Special is picking up speed as it proceeds east.

On the Atlantic City Division where the grate had been reduced, the method used was to disconnect six sections of shaking grate at the front end of the firebox. This portion of the grate was then covered with firebrick. Sometimes a sheet of steel was placed over the grate before laying the bricks so that there would be no cold air leaks, should any of the bricks become broken. On the New Jersey Division a similar method was used but the area covered with brick was less, so that all of the shaking part of the grate was still open and operable.

Tests on the Altoona test plant, and on the road resulted in this official pronouncement; "The practice of reducing the grate is found to be undesirable as the capacity of the locomotive for making steam is reduced, and little benefit in smoke reduction realised."

COMPARISON OF GRATES TESTED

Where tested	Area of grate in square feet	Relative area in per cent	Ratio of heating surface to grate area
Standard	55.5	100	41.8
New Jersey Division	39.5	71	58.7
Atlantic City Division	29.76	54	77.9

No. 126.

In effect 12.01 A.M. December 1st, 1907

STATIONS.

03	71	11	53	101	79	DISTANCE FROM NEW YORK	STATIONS.	102	18	52	14	10	80	6
Western & N'th'rn Mail	Federal Express	St. Louis Mail	Newspaper Special South	Phila. Accom.	New York and Southern Express.			Phila. and New York Accom.	Chicago Mail.	Mail and Express.	St. Louis Mail.	Eastern Express.	Atlantic Coast Line Express.	New York Express.
A.M.	A.M.	A.M.	A.M.	A.M.	A.M.			A.M.	A.M.	A.M.	A.M.	A.M.	A.M.	A.M.
				C12.10	C12.10		NEW YORK (23d St.)					S7.15	S7.30	S7.30
		E2.30	E2.00	C12.15	C12.15		NEW YORK (Desb. St.)	C3.53				S7.13	S7.23	S7.23
		E2.45	E2.05	C12.15	C12.15		NEW YORK (Cort. St.)	C3.53				S7.13	S7.23	S7.23
				C11.45	C11.45		BROOKLYN					S7.35	S7.35	S7.35
E4.45	4.10	E3.01	E2.26	C12.33	C12.30	1.0	JERSEY CITY	C3.38	C3.44	E5.05	E6.00	C6.55	C7.08	S7.10
E4.59	E4.23	3.12	E2.38	C12.50	E12.47	8.7	NEWARK	C3.16	3.31	E4.49	E5.45	C6.40	C6.52	C6.55
5.01	4.26	3.14	2.40	C12.53	C12.49	9.6	SOUTH ST. NEWARK	C3.10	3.29	4.46	5.43	6.36	6.49	6.51
5.03	4.28	3.15	2.42	12.55	12.52	10.3	W. NEWARK JUNC.	3.08	3.28	4.45	5.42	6.35	6.48	6.50
5.04	4.29	3.16	2.56	12.56	12.53	11.4	WAVERLY	3.07	3.27	4.44	5.41	6.34	6.47	6.49
5.08	4.31	3.19	2.45	C1.01	E12.58	11.1	ELIZABETH	C3.02	3.24	E4.40	5.37	C6.30	D6.43	6.45
5.15	4.38	3.24	2.51	C1.13	E1.10	19.4	RAHWAY	F2.49	3.18	E4.30	5.29	6.21	6.33	6.35
5.16	4.39	3.25	2.52	1.15	1.12	20.0	PERTH AMBOY JUNC	2.47	3.17	4.28	5.28	6.20	6.31	6.34
5.20	4.43	3.29	2.56	1.23	1.20	24.9	MENLO PARK	2.41	3.13	4.22	5.23	6.14	6.28	6.28
5.23	4.46	3.31	2.58	F1.27	1.24	25.8	METUCHEN	F2.37	3.10	4.19	5.21	C6.11	6.23	6.25
E5.30	4.53	3.36	3.03	C1.38	E1.34	31.3	NEW BRUNSWICK	C2.25	3.02	E4.11	5.14	C6.02	6.14	6.17
5.33	4.55	3.38	3.05	1.42	1.39	32.9	MILLSTONE JUNC	2.19	3.00	4.08	5.12	5.58	6.10	6.14
5.39	5.02	3.44	3.11	1.51	1.48	38.5	DEANS	2.09	2.54	4.00	5.06	5.51	6.01	6.08
5.42	5.05	3.47	3.14	1.56	1.53	41.0	MONMOUTH JUNC.	F2.04	2.51	3.57	5.01	5.48	5.57	6.05
E5.51	5.12	3.53	3.20	2.07	2.04	47.0	PRINCETON JUNC.	C1.53	2.44	3.49	4.55	5.42	5.49	5.59
5.57	5.17	3.57	3.24	2.13	2.10	51.2	LAWRENCE	1.45	2.39	3.43	4.50	5.37	5.43	5.54
E6.07	B5.25	4.04	E3.31	S2.24	E2.20	56.7	TRENTON	C1.35	2.31	E3.35	4.43	C5.29	E5.34	S5.45
6.09	5.28	4.06	3.33	2.28	2.23	58.0	MORRISVILLE	F1.25	2.28	3.30	4.40	5.26	5.29	5.42
6.15	5.34	4.11	3.38	2.37	2.32	63.1	TULLYTOWN	F1.13	2.22	3.24	4.34	5.19	5.24	5.36
6.20	5.38	4.15	3.43	F2.44	2.39	66.9	BRISTOL	F1.05	2.18	E3.20	4.30	5.15	5.19	5.32
6.27	5.45	4.20	3.48	2.54	2.49	72.4	CORNWELLS	F12.53	2.13	3.13	4.22	5.09	5.12	5.25
6.30	5.48	4.22	3.50	2.58	2.53	74.5	TORRESDALE	F12.47	2.11	3.11	4.20	5.06	5.09	E5.22
6.33	5.51	4.25	3.54	3.01	2.57	77.1	HOLMESBURG JUNC.	S12.40	2.08	3.08	4.17	5.03	5.06	5.18
6.37	5.55	4.29	3.58	3.07	3.04	80.8	FRANKFORD	S12.30	2.04	3.04	4.12	4.58	5.00	5.13
6.38	5.56	4.30	3.59	3.08	3.05	81.1	"F. J. TOWER"	12.27	2.03	3.03	4.11	4.57	4.59	5.12
6.41	6.00	4.33	4.02	3.13	3.10	83.8	NORTH PENN. JUNC.	F12.22	1.59	3.00	4.07	4.54	4.56	5.09
E6.44	D6.02	4.35	E4.05	B3.17	B3.14	84.9	NORTH PHILA	S12.20	1.57	E2.58	L4.05	E4.51	E4.53	X5.06
6.49	6.07	4.39	4.10	3.25	3.22	85.6	3 TOWER (Mantua)	12.11	1.52	2.53	4.00	4.46	4.48	5.01
6.52	D6.11	4.42	4.13	D3.29	B3.26	89.2	WEST PHILADELPHIA	C12.06		2.49		C4.42	C4.44	C4.57
E6.55	D6.15	E4.45	E4.17	S3.34		90.3	PHILADELPHIA	S12.02		E2.45		S4.33	S4.40	S4.53
A.M.	A.M.	A.M.	A.M.	A.M.	A.M.			A.M.	A.M.	A.M.	A.M.	A.M.	A.M.	A.M.

STATIONS.

309	311	305	303	467	301	DISTANCE FROM NEW YORK	STATIONS.	DISTANCE BETWEEN STATIONS	300	302	304	306	308	310
N. York & Waverly Accom.	N. York & Rahway Accom.	N. York & Waverly Accom.	N. York & Waverly Accom.	New York & Trenton Accom.	N. York & P. Amboy Accom.				Rahway & N. York Accom.	Rahway & N. York Accom.	P. Amboy & N. York Accom.	N. Bruns. & N. York Accom.	P. Amboy & N. York Accom.	Waverly & N. York & Accom.
A.M.	A.M.	A.M.	A.M.	A.M.	A.M.				A.M.	A.M.	A.M.	A.M.	A.M.	A.M.
S7.55	S7.25	S7.25	S6.25	S6.25			NEW YORK (23d St.)		S6.30	S7.00	S7.30	S7.45	S8.00	S8.15
S8.10	S7.40	S7.30	S6.40	S6.30	S6.00		NEW YORK (Desb. & Cort. Sts.)	1.0	S6.23	S6.53	S7.13	S7.33	S7.53	S8.13
S7.45	S7.15	S7.15	S6.15	S6.15			BROOKLYN		S6.35	S7.05	S7.35	S8.05	S8.05	S8.35
S8.24	S7.55	S7.48	S6.55	S6.44	S6.14	1.0	JERSEY CITY	2.3	S6.11	S6.41	S7.01	S7.21	S7.38	S7.56
S8.30	S8.01	S7.54	S7.01	S6.50	S6.19	3.3	MARION	4.8	S6.05	S6.35	S6.56	7.16	7.32	S7.50
S8.38	8.07	S8.00	S7.07	6.57	6.25	8.1	HARRISON	0.6	5.58	S6.25	6.49	7.09	7.26	S7.42
S8.41	S8.10	S8.02	S7.10	7.00	S6.28	8.7	NEWARK	0.9	S5.55	S6.22	S6.47	7.07	7.24	S7.39
S8.44	S8.13	S8.05	S7.13	S7.02	S6.30	9.6	SOUTH ST. NEWARK	0.7	S5.52	S6.19	S6.44	7.04	S7.21	S7.36
8.46	8.15	8.07	7.15	7.04	6.32	10.3	WEST NEWARK JUNC.	1.1	S6.50	6.17	6.42	7.02	7.19	7.34
S8.49	8.16	S8.10	S7.18	7.05	6.34	11.4	WAVERLY	1.6	5.49	6.16	6.41	7.01	7.18	S7.31
	F8.19			7.08	S6.37	13.0	NORTH ELIZABETH	1.1	F5.46	6.14	F6.38	6.59	F7.15	
	S8.22			7.10	S6.40	14.1	ELIZABETH	0.6	S5.44	6.12	S6.36	S6.56	7.13	
	F8.24			F7.12	S6.42	14.7	SOUTH ELIZABETH	2.6	5.41	S6.09	S6.33	6.54	S7.10	
	S8.29			F7.15	S6.47	17.3	LINDEN	2.1	S5.37	S6.04	S6.28	F6.50	S7.05	
	S8.33			S7.20	S6.53	19.4	RAHWAY	0.6	S5.33	S5.59	S6.24	S6.46	S7.00	
	S8.35			7.22	6.54	20.0	PERTH AMBOY JC.	3.1	S5.30	S5.56	6.22	6.44	6.58	
					C7.03	23.1	WOODBRIDGE	1.8			S6.13		S6.50	
					7.09	24.9	LONG BRCH. JUNC.	1.5			6.09		6.46	
					S7.15	26.4	PERTH AMBOY				S6.05		S6.43	
				F7.25		21.5	COLONIA	1.2			F6.41			
				S7.28		22.7	ISELIN	1.9			S6.39			
				S7.30		21.9	MENLO PARK	1.9			S6.36			
				S7.34		25.8	METUCHEN	3.1			S6.31			
				S7.39		29.9	STELTON	2.4			S6.26			
				S7.46		31.3	NEW BRUNSWICK	1.6			S6.22			
				7.50		32.9	MILLSTONE JUNC.	5.6				6.17		
				F7.50		38.5	DEANS	2.5						
				S8.05		41.0	MONMOUTH JUNC.	6.0						
				S8.17		47.0	PRINCETON JUNC.	4.2						
				F8.25		51.2	LAWRENCE	5.5						
							TRENTON							

A **portion** of the employes official timetable for the New York Division, effective December 1st, 1907. It shows distances in miles between main stations between New York, Jersey City terminal and Broad Street Station, Philadelphia. Trains 79 and 101 were known as "Owl" trains and often carried Philadelphians back home after viewing a theatrical performance in New York.

Jersey City, May 30, 1908.

Mr. F. P. Abercrombie,
    Superintendent, New York Division.

Mr. W. N. Bannard,
    Superintendent, Maryland Division.

COPY

Gentlemen:

    We, the committee appointed to investigate the conditions existing on foreign lines where runs of 200 miles or over are made by same locomotive and crew, beg leave to submit the following report, and in preparing the same we have endeavored to explain fully and clearly the conditions under which the locomotive crews work on the several railroads mentioned, and for convenience, each railroad or division of railroad is referred to on separate sheets.

    We started from Grand Central depot, New York, at 10:00 A. M. May 7th, arrived at New Haven 12:00 o'clock Noon, and called at the General Offices of the N. Y., N. H. & H. R. R., where we were introduced to the General Manager's chief clerk, (the General Manager being absent.) After stating our business he informed us the long distance runs of that railroad had been discontinued after having been in service one week, or from April 12th to 19th, 1908. He explained, however, this was not due to any objection on the part of the locomotive crews as to the number of miles run, but on account of the inconvenience to the men living at New Haven. The crews living at Boston desired the runs to be continued. We were furnished transportation and a permit to ride on the locomotives.

(2)

NEW YORK, NEW HAVEN & HARTFORD RAILROAD.

Date, May 7th and 8th, 1908.

From Stamford to Boston.

Distance 198 Miles.

Schedule Time,-Average 5 hours.

Number of stops made,-not less than 5.

Average number of cars per train,-7.

Type of locomotive,- Atlantic & Pacific.

Fire-grate area,- 54 square feet for both types.

Kind of coal used,- Westmoreland gas.

Tender coal capacity., 28,000 pounds.

Average amount consumed per trip., 16,000 pounds.

Is coal taken en route? None.

Is fireman inconvenienced? No.

Tender water capacity,- 6,000 gallons.

Water taken en route,- twice from stand pipes.

Rate of pay,- Engineman 3-85/100 cents per mile.

  " " " Fireman 2-3/10 "   "   "

Hours off duty before making the return trip,-Cannot say owing to runs being discontinued.

Hours off duty at home end of road,- Cannot say on account of runs being discontinued.

Character of road,- generally level.

  "   " Signals., Hall electric and Manual block. Poorly arranged.

(3)

REMARKS

NEW YORK, NEW HAVEN & HARTFORD RAILROAD.

    On this division no trouble is experienced due to hot driving wheel boxes, which is attributed to the use of hard grease lubrication. Stops of five minutes duration is made at New London and Providence where water is taken and also where the coal in tender is shoveled forward by two men, so as to be convenient for the fireman. Locomotives on this division are regularly assigned. This railroad is all double track.

    It will be noted in introductory remarks the long distant runs were discontinued. They have, however, at present, several trains running between New Haven and Boston and return, a distance of 318 Miles, which are run by same locomotive and crew with a layover of two hours at Boston, during which time they back their trains down to South Boston, and crew is only off locomotive about 30 minutes, making their actual time on the trip 8 hours and 50 minutes.

    Locomotive crews advised us they much preferred the long runs, but owing to the inconvenience to men living at New Haven they requested that the runs be discontinued.

(4)

ATCHISON, TOPEKA & SANTA FE RAILROAD.

Date, May 12th, 1908.

From Chicago to Ft. Madison.

Distance, 237 Miles.

Division,- Illinois.

Schedule time,- 5 hours and 35 minutes.

Number of stops made,- 5.

Average number of cars per train,- 7.

Type of locomotive.- (Baldwin Balanced Compound) Atlantic.

Fire-grate area,- 49-1/2 square feet.

Kind of coal used., Illinois gas.

Tender coal capacity,- 24,000 pounds.

Average amount consumed during trip., 16,000 pounds.

Is coal taken en route? Once.

Is fireman inconvenienced? No.

Tender water capacity., 8,500 gallons.

Water taken en route,- three times from stand pipes.

Rate of pay., Enginemen 4 cents per mile

  "   "   " Firemen 2-5/10 cents per mile

Hours off duty before making return trip,- See remarks "A".

Hours off duty at home end of road,-See remarks "A".

Character of road,-Level except one grade 7 miles long of 1 per cent.

Character of signals., Manual semaphore, spaced several miles apart.

These Crews make 10 round trips per month.

13

GRAND RAPIDS & INDIANA RAILROAD.

Date May 19th, 1908.

From Grand Rapids to Mackinaw City.

Distance, 226 Miles.

Schedule time,- 9 hours.

Number of stops made,- 82 regular.

Average number of cars per train,- 6.

Type of locomotive,- Baldwin 10 wheel.

Fire grate area,- 28 square feet.

Kind of coal used,- Ohio gas.

Tender coal capacity,- 22,000 pounds.

Average amount consumed per trip,-22,000 pounds.

Is coal taken en route? Once.

Is fireman inconvenienced? No.

Tender water capacity,- 4,500 gallons.

Water taken en route,- 3 times from stand pipes.

Rate of pay,- Enginemen $8.35 per trip.

" " " Firemen   4.10 "   "

Hours off duty before making return trip,- 15.

" " " home end of road,- 64, see remarks "A".

Character of road,- Very hilly. There is one grade of 1-1/2 per cent 9 miles long south of Petoskey.

Character of signals,- Manual semaphore order boards.

14

REMARKS

GRAND RAPIDS & INDIANA RAILROAD.

On this division very little locomotive detention due to hot driving-wheel boxes is experienced/ which are oil boxes. This may be attributed to local service.

Locomotives on this division are all pooled.

There are several railroad crossings at grade but not positive as to the exact number of them. There are 217 miles of single and 9 miles of double track.

A stop of 20 minutes is made at Cadillac in both directions for dinner. This is only time that the locomotive crew is off engine during trip.

The crews are required to get telegraphic orders or clearance cards at every block signal station.

"A". The locomotive crews at present make only 7 round trips owing to depression of business and lay over 64 hours at home end of road each trip. In normal conditions they make ten round trips per month and lay over 40 hours at home end of road each trip.

Owing to character of the road the number of hours of service and the number of stops made, these runs are particularly taxing physically.

These locomotive crews were cheerful and much preferred long runs over short runs.

This is engine No. 2766, that pulled J. P. Morgan's Special train over the New York Division, between West Philadelphia and Manhattan Transfer, at an average speed of 67.4 mph, on January 23, 1911. No. 2766 was a locomotive of the E2a class, built at Juniata Shops in 1905. It is shown here pulling the eastbound Manhattan Limited, train No. 22 in 1909. First car is an all-steel Railway Post Office car, class M70. Other cars are of wooden construction.

This is a black and white copy of the beautiful and enormous colored photograph on thick glass, that used to adorn the northern wall of the Arcade in Penn Station years ago among others. It was another of Wm. H. Rau's photographs, and was blown up to such large proportions that the engine number which was 1610 was plainly discernible on the headlight and smokebox number plate. Underneath the picture were the words ''First All-Steel 18-Hour Train Between New York And Chicago.'' My understanding is that this picture was taken in 1910 quite a few months before Penn Station in New York was opened. Engine 1610 was of the E3a class built in 1904. It was frequently assigned to trains 28 and 29, the east and westbound sections of the Pennsylvania Special, respectively. Train had just crossed the Delaware River from the Trenton side, and running west was entering Bucks County, Pa. near Morrisville station. Train consist was six cars, and remained so for sometime afterwards. Dining car was dropped at Altoona, and another one picked up the following morning at Alliance, Ohio, for the remainder of the run to Chicago.

A good view of the standard lightweight Walschaerts gear used on classes E2d and E3d Atlantics. Also shown is the ''gooseneck'' reachrod and roller which indicates that the reverse lever is set for backward motion. Axel Vogt's vacuum relief valve is enclosed by the casing on top of the valve chest. Baldwin's simplified spring equalization design introduced by them on class E28, between the rear drivers and trailing wheels was speedily adopted and made standard on classes E2d and E3d. Clearly shown under one of the main air reservoirs is the long equalizing beam with slotted openings to reduce weight. Safety strap at end of Vogt crosshead guides was good insurance to prevent derailment in event of main rod breaking from crosshead pin. Pennsy used safety straps on their passenger locomotives for many years. Engine 3158 class E2d built in 1906, was waiting for train 22, which changed engines and crews at ''3'' Tower around 1907-1908. This interlocking tower at Mantua Junction was near a spot quaintly known as ''Keg Park'' due to its proximity to Brewerytown in Philadelphia.

21

Jersey City, May 30th, 190 .

Mr. F. P. Abercrombie,
        Superintendent, New York Division.

Mr. W. N. Bannard,
        Superintendent, Maryland Division.

Gentlemen:
            Supplementary our report of even date, we, the com-
mittee appointed to investigate the conditions existing on railroads
having long distant runs of 200 miles or more for locomotives and
crews, desire to show our appreciation of the kind and courteous
treatment for the special effort on the part of the officials of
the several railroads furnishing us the desired information, and
we respectfully ask, if consistent, a letter of thanks be extended
to them.

        New York, New Haven & Hartford, Atchison, Topeka & Santa Fe,
Chicago, Rock Island & Pacific, Chicago Great Western and Grand
Rapids & Indiana Railroads.

        We further desire to call attention to the kindness of Mr.
W. H. Scriven, Supt. & Genl. Manager of Chicago Terminal, his
chief clerk, Mr. Jones; also Mr. McGraw, Road Foreman of Engines,
who accompanied us on our visit idfferent railroads in Chicago.
We also desire to commend the enginemen and firemen with whom we
rode over the several railroads, as we found them cheerful employes,
very proficient in their work; all of the enginemen being particularly expert in handling the air brake, and firemen experts in
firing their locomotives.

22

Yours very truly,

                    (W. P. Garrabrant.
                    (
                    (F. Linthicum.
        COMMITTEE   (
                    (Martin H. Lee.
                    (
                    (W. T. Bailey.

1

Jersey City, N. J., June 9, 1908.

Mr. F. P. Abercrombie,
    Superintendent, New York Division.

Dear Sir:
            Referring to report under date of June 1st, sub-
mitted by committee appointed to investigate conditions existing on foreign lines where runs of 200 miles or over are
made by the same locomotive and crew, beg leave to submit
the following expression of our opinion:

        In comparing conditions on foreign lines with those on
the New York and Maryland Divisions, and after taking everything
into consideration, believe the runs between Jersey City and
Washington can be made by the same locomotive and crew without
hardship or inconvenience to the men, as in our judgment, we
consider the numerous telegraphic orders received on single
track lines are far more taxing mentally than any conditions
existing on the line between Jersey City and Washington.

        The time consumed in making runs of this character on
foreign lines being so much greater than that consumed on the
New York and Maryland Divisions, we do not consider the phys-
ical tax any comparison.

        Viewing the conditions existing from the firemen's
stand-point, we consider there should be no inconvenience
whatever experienced, as the tender coal capacity is ample.
It will be necessary, however, to have the tender properly

(2)

loaded before leaving the terminal.

        In conclusion we desire to add that in our judgment
better results generally will be obtained by installing the long
distance runs for locomotive crews between Jersey City and Washington.

            Yours respectfully,

    (SIGNED) W. P. Garabrant
                    Asst.Road Foreman of Engines N.Y.Div.
    (SIGNED) F. Linthicum
                    Asst.Road Foreman of Engines Md.Div.
    (SIGNED) Martin H. Lee
                    Engineman, New York Division.
    (SIGNED) W. T. Bailey
                    Fireman, Maryland Division.

Chapter 6
Signals and Safety

Safety with speed with emphasis on safety was a credo of the Pennsy. To achieve this they spared no expense and in 1902 they equipped 87 miles of the New York Division, and part of the Philadelphia Division, with the automatic block system, which according to the Pennsy rule book represented "A series of consecutive blocks, governed by block signals, operated by electric, pneumatic or other agency actuated by a train, or certain conditions affecting the use of a block." A block was a length of track of defined limits, the use of which by trains was governed by block signals.

It was back in 1879 that initial action was taken to establish a signal department on the Pennsy. H. F. Cox, of the Motive Power department was placed in charge of signal work on December 1st of that year. Assigned to assist Cox was George D. Fowle, also of the same department. With two other Motive Power department men, Fowle supervised the installation of the first large interlocking plant at Broad Street Station in 1881. For his fine work on this project Fowle received a $100 gratuity from the railroad. On June 11, 1883, H. F. Cox was appointed Engineer of Signals, reporting to William H. Brown, Chief Engineer. Lines West of Pittsburgh followed suit and also established a Signal Department in 1886.

H. F. Cox was succeeded by George D. Fowle, as Engineer of Signals on August 1, 1887. But it was 1883 which can be considered the official date of a Pennsylvania Railroad Signal Department, and regarded as the oldest in America. Exactly twenty years later, August 1, 1907, A. H. Rudd became Signal Engineer, and in March 1920, became Chief Signal Engineer of the entire Pennsylvania System.

Prior to 1902, automatic block signals had been in partial use on the New York and Philadelphia Divisions. These were placed on wooden masts or brackets, but in anticipation of an increase in traffic, especially high-speed passenger trains, due in great part to their plans for a direct rail entrance into New York City, they enlarged and greatly improved the former arrangement. Steel bridges, masts and brackets replaced those of wood as far west as Paoli, Pa. about 104 miles, for the support of the semaphores.

Most of the railroad between Jersey City and Philadelphia on the New York Division was four tracked, and sturdy signal bridges which spanned those tracks were used. But on the road between Overbrook, or "OB" tower to Paoli, bracket-post signals were used. The reason for this arrangement was plain economy. This was a heavily traveled commuter line, and with stations close together (one station for every mile the men used to say) it was desired to locate the signals in the most suitable spot for starting semaphores at the stations. At any station a train headed east or west had a signal not far in front of it, and with a train standing at a station it was always a good distance in front of the home automatic signal which protected it at the rear.

With this arrangement and desire to have signals placed as described, to use much costlier signal bridges supporting just two signal masts with their attendant semaphores on each bridge would have been economically unsound.

Typical bracket-post signal used by Pennsy from Philadelphia to Paoli. Signal on eastbound track No. 1, is in "stop" position, while signal semaphores on freight track No. 2, give a "clear" indication. Passenger train on left is a Paoli local hauled by D16a class engine No. 96, which hauled the Pennsylvania Special on its first Westbound trip June 15, 1902, between Powelton Avenue Station in West Philadelphia, to Harrisburg, Pa. A plodding H6a is on the westbound freight track No. 3, and climbing the grade as it passes Narberth, Pa. in 1907.

Where traffic was heavy as on the New York Division, and the line to Paoli, the automatic block signal system was much favored. By its action the train service was practically controlled by the passage of the trains themselves. When one train entered a block it set the signal behind it at "danger" and the one in the rear of this signal at "caution" thereby, giving the engineer of a following train time to bring down his speed to a point where he could stop before passing the danger signal.

Operation of these New York and Philadelphia Division signals of the automatic block system was by the Westinghouse electro-pneumatic method. Its essential feature was an electric current flowing through the track rails. The signal being at the entrance of a block section, insulated at both ends from the adjoining block sections, which was, say three-quarters of a mile long, (this varied according to local and traffic conditions) the battery for the current was at the outgoing end; and when the rails throughout the section, and also the rails of the side tracks and crossovers, so far as they fouled the main track, were clear,—not occupied by wheels at any point,—the circuit of the battery was through the right-hand rail of the track to the electro-magnet of the signal, thence to the left-hand rail and by that to the battery. That circuit being closed, the electro-

magnet at the signal was energized and held the signal, through the medium of a stronger electro-magnet, worked by a lock battery in the all-clear or go-ahead position. The entrance of a train short circuited the current through the wheels and axles, de-energizing the electro-magnet, and the signal, by force of gravity, assumed the stop position, or aspect, thus warning the next following train not to enter the section. The signal remained at stop until every pair of wheels had passed out of the section.

The lower arm on each post was always a distant or cautionary signal, informing the engineman of the position of the "home" or stop signal at the entrance of the next succeeding block section. This provision was made for the purpose of avoiding loss of time during fogs, or whenever the engineer could not see a stop signal until he came within a short distance of it. The distant signal gave him notice at least a block ahead of the position of the home signal, whether or not he was to be stopped by it, so that in spite of fog or darkness he could run at a high speed, provided he could come to a stop in the space between the signals. The distant signal was controlled by the movement of the corresponding "home" through the medium of a wire on poles; or by means of a polarized relay, it could be controlled by the track circuit of the section between the home and its corresponding distant signal. This did away with the line wires and obviated certain disturbances by lightning.

The power for moving the arm to the downward or all-clear position was compressed air, of about 70 pounds pressure per square inch, acting through a cylinder fixed in an iron box at the foot of the signal mast. The pneumatic pressure was conveyed from a compressor to several signals along the line, for a distance of 10 to 20 miles, by means of an iron pipe buried in the ground. In moving a semaphore arm, the air entering the cylinder at its upper end forced down a piston which by its lever pushed up the signal rod inside the cylindrical iron mast and, thereby, moved the arm of the signal downward.

On releasing the pressure which occurred when a train entered the block section, the signal arm flew to the horizontal or stop position by gravity, a counterweight on its left-hand end, with the vertical rod inside the post, accomplishing this. An accidental failure of air pressure would have the same effect, throwing the signal to the stop position, thus bringing to a stand any train which might come along, and compelling the engineman to report the cause of the failure, which the inspector then checked out and removed.

The air cylinder was kept charged by means of an electro-magnet valve. This was operated by merely closing the track circuit. The de-energizing of the magnet on the entrance of a train was due to the fact that nearly all of the electric current flowed from one rail to the other through the wheels and axles of the cars as previously noted.

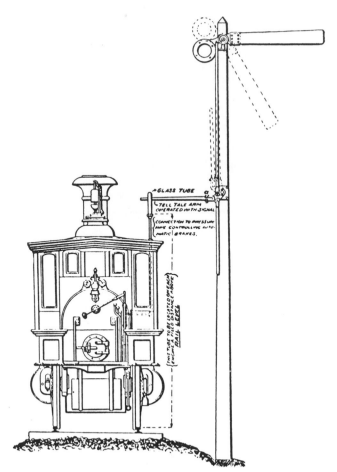

The Vogt automatic train stop, an early invention

An E2d Atlantic bound for Broad Street passes through West Philadelphia. It has just passed under the large six-track signal bridge seen in the background. The semaphore blades are all lower quadrant, which with the wooden cars hauled by the engine dates this scene to a period between 1906 and 1910.

Engine 2772, class E2a, built in 1905, approaching Narberth Station, on the long curve between that station and Merion Station to the east. Signals are clear for train 29, the Pennsylvania Special, as George Z. Gray, fireman, looks right at the camera. From the position of signal on track 4, No. 29 will soon be catching up with a Paoli local which is evidently not too far ahead. The "Special" is running around the slower train. Bracket-post signals A-16 and A-17, are for eastbound and westbound traffic respectively. The letter "A" indicated "automatic" block signals actuated automatically by the train's passage. The top blade with the straight-edge end, was the "home" signal, and the lower fish-tail blade was the "distant" signal. Each blade only used two positions, either a horizontal one, or dropping to a 45 degree downward angle.

In night service the indication of a clear block could be given by showing a white light on the semaphore mast. When the arm of a home signal assumed the horizontal or danger position, a red glass was set in front of the light. On a number of railroads the all-clear aspect was replaced by green in place of white, and in such cases the distant signal also showed green for all-clear, while for the caution indication the distant signal was made to show on some roads, yellow, and on others a combination of red and green, a red light and a green light being fixed close together, side by side.

As pointed out when these semaphore signals were installed, white was the color that denoted a "clear" aspect. Around 1908, green began to appear as the "clear" aspect. This change was due in great part to vandalism by target-practice huntsmen, and others intent upon, as the railroad put it, "malicious mischief." These vandals would shoot or stone out

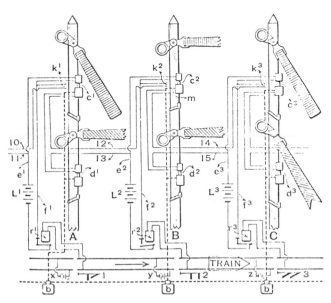

Electric Circuits for Electro-Pneumatic Block Signals

General principle of the automatic block system on the Pennsy, showing three signal aspects. Two of the signals have already been affected by the train's passage.

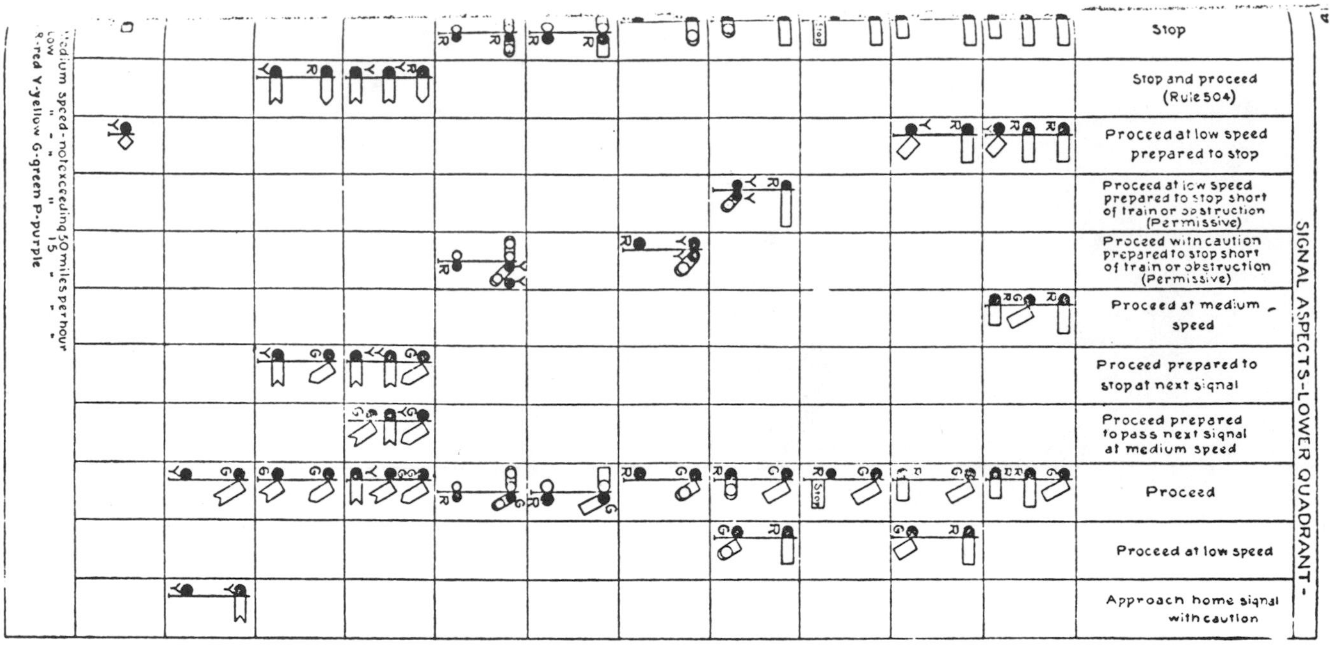

Aspects of lower quadrant signals used on Pennsy main lines up to 1912-1913. From Sunnyside Yards to Manhattan Transfer, but on the Pennsylvania Tunnel and Terminal Railroad Company, upper quadrant signals with color light signals in the tunnels, Penn Station, and a few at the Transfer, were used on the initial installation in 1910.

A big K2, No. 3345, built in 1911, at Juniata, picks up speed shortly after leaving North Philadelphia Station in 1911. Train is No. 40, the Cincinnati-New York Express with all-steel equipment. Engineer is Ollie Keller of Harrisburg, Pa., and for some time he ran this train east and the Pennsylvania Special west. As can be seen this train undoubtedly would have been too much for any of the light Atlantics, and the costlier expediency of doubleheading would have been required. In the background is the old style signal bridge truss as are the lower quadrant signals supported upon it. A class D16b engine is running westbound on track 4, heading, quite possibly, a Bristol-Philadelphia local. Note the contrast in size between the two locomotives. One thing they had in common; both used saturated (non-superheated) steam. In 1912, however, the Pennsy applied superheaters to some existing locomotives, and the policy from then on was to equip all new road power with superheaters.

The signal chart shows the following aspect meanings (right column):

- Stop
- Stop and proceed (Rule 504)
- Proceed at low speed prepared to stop
- Proceed at low speed prepared to stop short of train or obstruction (Permissive)
- Proceed with caution prepared to stop short of train or obstruction (Permissive)
- Proceed at medium speed
- Proceed prepared to stop at next signal
- Proceed prepared to pass next signal at medium speed
- Proceed
- Proceed at low speed
- Approach home signal with caution

SIGNAL ASPECTS - LOWER QUADRANT -

Legend: medium speed - not exceeding 50 miles per hour — low - 15 - ; R-red Y-yellow G-green P-purple the signal blades colored glass roundels. Thus if the signal showed "red" for danger it would appear white or clear, quite a dangerous situation if the danger signal was protecting a train a short distance ahead, and hidden by a curve. But with all lights colored, a white light meant "stop and investigate" at close range by the position of the semaphore blade. This was an advantage over later day color light signals which depended wholly upon the lights and could not be checked by a signal blade's position. Today, with cab signals, wayside signals have in certain locations been discontinued, as wayside relays alone visibly show the engine crew conditions ahead of them in the cab.

Nevertheless, there was nothing wrong about the visibility of a white light. For as Martin Lee observed when running over the western plains, white signals at night could be seen further than any other color. Red was next in brightness for a good distance, but yellow and green were the poorest of all and disappeared in about one mile. He made these observations from the rear platform of a passenger train.

The Pennsy experimented with upper quadrant signals in 1907, and the newly electrified line between Manhattan Transfer, and Sunnyside Yards used them exclusively. In the tunnels and Penn Station, New York, color light signals prevailed, as did a few special signals at Manhattan transfer.

With passing years new bridges on the New York Division were erected using Warren type trusses to support the semaphores, but the older style bridges were still in use on the Division and elsewhere. Later many of these bridges had position light signals upon them especially when the line began operation of electric powered passenger trains between New York and Philadelphia on January 16, 1933. In the meantime many truss bridges had been replaced by "beam" type form, and a number of truss bridges built on the massive side acted as "anchor" bridges for the catenary system were enabled to resist the stresses imposed.

Between Overbrook and Paoli, position light signals were used when the line began electrified passenger train operation for the 20 miles between Broad Street Station and Paoli, on September 12, 1915. Due to their shape these were called "tombstone" signals and several lights against a black metal background gave aspects to simulate the movement of a semaphore blade. Later the shape of the black background was changed, but using the same arrangement of lights to represent each semaphore movement. Finally, a circular standard design with fewer lights was used and is still standard on the Pennsy.

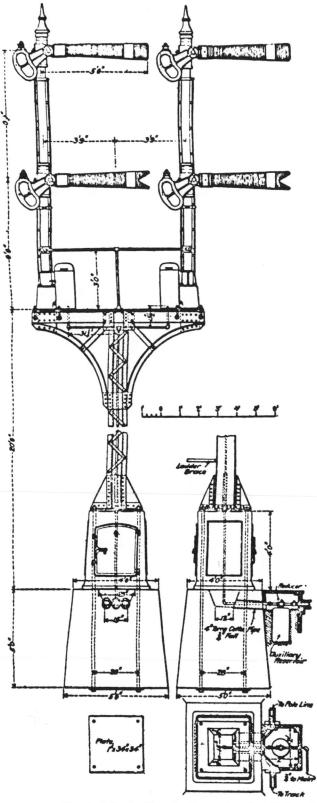

-Bracket-Post Signal—Pennsylvania Railroad, Philadelphia Division.

Signal masts showing shape of blades and mechanism used by the Pennsy on bridges and bracket-post structures.

Engine No. 1610, class E3a, built at Juniata in 1904, passing signals at Radnor, Pa., around 1909. At the right is a signal mast with three semaphore blades which permitted four signal indications instead of three. This gave fast through trains which frequently ran on the inside tracks more "searoom" in case of an obstruction ahead of them. The outside tracks were quite busy with Paoli locals, and at times faster trains had to "run around them." This train from its consist appears to be the Manhattan Limited, which carried the mail in a car of its own. First car is an all-steel M70 class, Railway Post Office Car, second is a wooden Pullman Combination Car, as can be seen by the truss rods under the car body. Third car is an all-steel D70 class Dining Car, and the last two are wooden Pullmans, a Sleeping Car, and Observation-Compartment-Sleeping Car, in that order. Engine 1610 of the Philadelphia Division, was honored by being pictured in a gigantic colored "blow-up" glass photograph displayed in Penn Station arcade. I never walked by it without looking at it, and enjoying the realistic impression of a moving train hauled by a Pennsy Atlantic. In Chapter 5, is a picture in black and white that duplicates the Penn Station photo. The only difference is that engine 1610 in this book is running with a "clean" stack, but in the arcade picture I believe someone "faked in" a very low flat trailing line of smoke from the stack to impart the impression of terrific speed. To have attained such an effect in reality, with an open throttle the locomotive would probably have had to be traveling at about 100-mph.

Years before the twentieth century automatic train stops entered into the subject of signaling, and many were the varied and sometimes weird methods used to prevent a train from passing a stop signal. Axel Vogt invented such a device in collaboration with J. Wood, also of the Motive Power Department and had them applied to several locomotives running on the Middle Division in 1880. This contrivance was effective enough, but a glass tube which formed part of its construction was just too delicate for workaday railroading, and a frequency of undesired stops caused its discontinuance.

Trains running through the East and North River tunnels were protected by color-light signals and electro-pneumatic trip stops. As these trains were electrically operated the controller's deadman feature provided additional protection. Today we have wayside signals reproduced in the cab of the locomotive or multiple-unit car. Instant telephonic communication between engineman and interlocking tower is also used.

But semaphore signals have given way to color light and position light signals. Nonetheless, the old semaphores gave a colorful touch to railroading and their role in preventing accidents deserves a tribute.

Engine 96, class D16a, built at Juniata in 1897, on its first west-bound trip with the Pennsylvania Special. Train had just passed Merion Station, Pa., and the contrast in the roles 96 is playing is interesting. One day you head the road's top-name train, and then —a Paoli local. Tender coupled to 96 when hauling the "Special" has a flared collar which was applied to these earlier D16a class engines.

Train No. 28, the Pennsylvania Special headed by E2 class engine 1973, built in 1901 at Juniata, speeds over Neshaminy Creek and passes under signal bridge 444. This was the original numbering, but later the numerals represented miles west of a fixed point in the Cortlandt Street Ferry Station, New York City. On this day Ollie Keller was the engineer and George Z. Gray, the fireman. These bridges were standard on the New York Division except for a short distance west of North Philadelphia—or Germantown Junction when they were put in service in 1902.

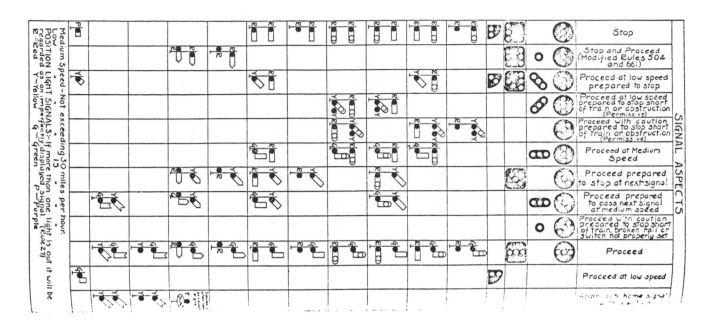

	SIGNAL ASPECTS
	Stop
	Stop and Proceed (Modified Rules 504 and 661)
	Proceed at low speed prepared to stop
	Proceed at low speed prepared to stop short of train or obstruction (Permissive)
	Proceed with caution prepared to stop short of train or obstruction (Permissive)
	Proceed at Medium Speed
	Proceed prepared to stop at next signal
	Proceed prepared to pass next signal at medium speed
	Proceed with caution prepared to stop short of train, broken rail or switch not properly set
	Proceed
	Proceed at low speed
	approach home signal

Left margin vertical text: Medium Speed—Not exceeding 30 miles per hour. Low 15. POSITION LIGHT SIGNALS:—If more than one light is out it will be regarded as an imperfectly displayed signal (Rule 27). R—Red Y—Yellow G—Green P—Purple

Signal aspects for upper quadrant signals as used on the Pennsy after discontinuance of lower quadrant type signals. Position light signals as used today are also illustrated.

Bridge structure as used in 1902 supports upper quadrant signals as train No. 11, westbound St. Louis-Southwestern Mail passes under it. Train is climbing grade leading to Horseshoe Curve, and pulled by an M1 class engine No. 6884, built by Baldwin in September 1926. Two upper quadrant single-bladed automatic semaphores are governing movement on two westbound tracks 3 and 4, but each semaphore provides three aspects formerly using two blades per track. Tracks 1 and 2, for eastbound traffic and each signal mast has two automatic signals which provide four signal aspects each. Tracks 1 and 2, are on a descending grade and as mentioned in another caption need plenty of "searoom" or stopping space in case of a blocked track ahead. Pointed blades represent automatic block signals operated by train and track circuit. Number on this specific bridge 2410, shows that the bridge is 241.0 miles west of Broad Street Station, Philadelphia.

Chapter 7
Bigger and Better

As we have seen in Chapter 4, the Pennsy went to the Pacific type in 1907. Its fine performance proved its superiority over the smaller Atlantics and indicated its ability to not only meet the needs of the moment, but of those anticipated for the future.

The Fort Wayne drawing room of the Motive Power Department modified the Alco experimental class K28 and brought it closer to Pennsy standards and practice. Externally this was evident in the use of the Belpaire firebox and straight-line running boards with a relocation of the main air brake reservoirs on both sides of the locomotive. The result was class K2.

This was quite possibly the largest Pacific type engine then in operation on an American railroad, and it used saturated (non-superheated) steam. It gave the Pennsy "big" power when they quickly needed it successfully meeting the service requirements despite steel car consists and fast schedules. Mr. James T. Wallis former Chief of Motive Power of the Pennsylvania Railroad, Lines East and West, informed the writer personally that the K2 Pacifics gave most satisfactory service. They were, however, not a "home town" or Altoona product, and thus on the road east of Pittsburgh were sometimes referred to disparagingly. But they certainly were a blessing to the Pennsy in their hour of travail before the coming of the super E6s class Atlantics or the famous K4s class Pacifics. Otherwise much costly doubleheading would have been necessary to meet traffic demands for some time to come.

In the meantime, Alfred W. Gibbs, General Superintendent of Motive Power, at Altoona, had been working on the possibility of a super Atlantic. Together with his able assistants, Axel Vogt, Mechanical Engineer, and William F. Kiesel, Jr., Assistant Mechanical Engineer, an Atlantic No. 5075, was produced in December 1910, that proved outstanding in its operation when pitted against the larger and heavier K2 class engines. At high speeds it actually outperformed the saturated steam K2's, and only was surpassed by a superheated K2sa class locomotive. This latter class was a K2 with some modifications, and was built as a K2a class engine. It is interesting to note that one of the K2 engines surpassed by the hand-fired E6 was stoker-fired. This testing which took place on the Fort Wayne route made plain that a superheated E6s would at high speeds surpass the saturated steam K2 class handily and in level territory equal or better the superheated K2s class.

From 1910 and 1911, Juniata Shops and Alco were turning out K2 class Pacifics. The Alco engines worked on Lines West on the Fort Wayne and Panhandle routes, though in World War 2, some may have operated east of Pittsburgh on the Pennsy and Long Island Rail Road as did some K3s class engines. I have seen such latter class engines in commuter service between Philadelphia and Wilmington, Delaware. Class K2 was built consecutively through the years 1910 to 1913. In that latter year Baldwin built thirty locomotives practically duplicating class K2sa excepting that they had 26 × 26 inch cylinders. All were equipped with superheaters and the Crawford mechanical stoker. This was of the underfeed type and produced almost smokeless combustion as the coal was literally coked before burning.

One of the earliest K2 class engines built at Juniata in 1910. Saturated steam was first used on these big Pacifics until late in 1911 when experimental applications of the Schmidt superheater were made on two locomotives of class K2. Later all K2 engines were superheated. The tender of this engine No. 150, was known as class 70P70c and measured 14 feet, 8 inches, between truck centers. It was later replaced by the low-sided class 70P66 which measured 17 feet, 8 inches between truck centers. There is a strong probability that after the shorter Atlantics it was thought the long-legged Pacifics might experience trouble at turntables and in clearing switches at some spots; thus many of the earlier K2 engines particularly on Lines West were coupled to the shorter tenders with the raised tank collars.

While the E6 of 1910 was going through its meta-morphosis, attention was being directed to passenger train operation on the Pittsburgh Division. Here heavy grades are encountered to this day, and Mr. Gibbs never intended his large boilered Atlantic for that section of the Pennsy. Something with more tractive force than a K2 was needed. The problem was handed over to Alco at Schenectady, and they came up with a huge Pacific No. 3395, class K29s. It was equipped with a Schmidt superheater, as it was called in those days, in deference to its inventor Dr. Wilhelm Schmidt, a German engineer who had spent years in developing the superheater. It was also applied to the additional two E6s class engines built in 1912 and to all of this class in 1914. At that time the suffix letter "s" meant the use of a super-heater. The K29s class engine was also fitted with a Crawford mechanical stoker. This big Pacific proved its ability to outhaul two light Atlantics, and laid the groundwork for the famous K4s class which fol-lowed. Many of its principal components were em-bodied in the K4s.

But even before the construction of the K29s Pacific in November, 1911, the Pennsy had begun to investigate the use of superheated steam on their engines. In fact, as far back as 1909 they had applied a Baldwin smokebox superheater to one of their Con-solidation type locomotives, No. 2846, class H6b. Primarily the advantage of superheating derived from its ability to provide a substantial decrease in water and fuel consumption, and an increase in

the boiler's steaming capacity. This in turn meant a corresponding increase in the locomotive's sus-tained hauling capacity.

The smokebox form of superheater in theory appeared very desirable, for it only used "waste heat" while retaining the original heating surface of the boiler. But the Schmidt "A" type firetube superheater while decreasing the heating surface through the use of large flues, gave a much higher degree of superheat and brought the steam to a greater gaseous state, thereby, giving an added "kick" to the cylinders pistons. Technically put, it was thermodynamically superior, for it enabled the locomotive to do more work on less coal and water—an excellent criteria and reason for its use.

In 1914, eighty E6s class engines were built at Juniata and came on the road. They embodied the final and excellent proportions that had been de-veloped on the three pilot models Nos. 5075 (later No. 1067) 89 and 1092. These three engines were in turn later revamped to conform to the arrange-ment and measurements of the 1914 classic Atlantics of that day.

When these locomotives appeared they were a magnificent sight to behold. And could those E6s engines steam. It used to be said that you could light four candles and place each one in a corner of the firebox and get up enough steam to take a train from Philadelphia to Manhattan Transfer! One fireman said that when you put a shovelful of coal on the fire the boiler pressure gauge went up five points. Nevertheless, exaggerations aside, a good fireman was always needed to get the best out of a steam locomotive, particularly on a hand-fired job. Tractive force and horsepower formulas and weighty engineering department prognostications amount to little if the fireman is unseasoned, or working with a tank of poor coal which, despite careful checking did get dumped into the tender occasionally. To get a detailed story of the background, design, construction, and operation of the class E6s engines of the Pennsy, the reader may find much of interest in the book "APEX OF THE ATLANTICS" by Frederick Westing. Published by Kalmbach Publishing Co. 1027 N. Seventh St. Milwaukee, Wis. 53233.

But one thing for sure, Alfred Gibbs was convinced that a specially designed locomotive should be built for passenger service on the rugged terrain of the Pittsburgh Division. He had held to this belief long before the coming of Alco's K29s Pacific going back to the days when double and triple headers of light Atlantics curved around the sinuous ribbons of steel approaching Horseshoe Curve from the east and west. In fact he had prepared a preliminary design for such an engine of the Pacific type. It was even given a class K1 classification and would have used 26 × 26 inch cylinders with 72 inch drivers.

It might be said, however, that two of Mr. Gibbs salient points achieved reality in class K2sb class of which two Nos. 3370 and 3375 were built with 72 inch drivers. Also in class K3s which while using 80 inch drivers did use to advantage the 26 × 26 inch cylinders proposed by Gibbs. Later classes M1 and M1a appeared with 72 inch drivers and 27 × 30 inch cylinders and operated in passenger and freight service on the Pittsburgh Division. In 1900 the Pennsy built some G4 class passenger locomotives for use on the Pittsburgh Division. They were of the 4-6-0 type and used 72 inch drivers. Although these engines developed greater tractive force than the D16 class Americans in use at the time, they failed to supplant them. Some were used on the Pittsburgh Division, but most ran west of that point.

C. T. 220
6x16½ 2000M 3-16-2

PENNSYLVANIA RAILROAD SYSTEM

REPORT OF CARS ON PASSENGER TRAIN

(A) To __FDD__ (B) From __Phila.__ (C) __Nov. 17 1923__

(D) ____ Sec. of (F) __2__ Arr. (G) ____ M. Left (H) __321p__

(J) Engine __169__ (E6s) with Cars in following order from Engine

Kind of Car	Number or Name of Car	Point of Origin	Final Destination
(K)	(M)	(N)	(O)
1 Sl.	Haverford	Chgo.	New York
2 Pl.	Avondale	Pgh.	"
3 Dn.	4418	"	"
4 Sl.	Lenover	Chgo.	"
5 "	Simonides	"	"
6 Plb.	Watsontown	"	"
7			
8			
9			
10			
11			
12			
13			
14			
15			
16			
Total Number of Cars 6 cars			

(Q) Conductor __Prizor__   (R) Engineman __Frank Howard__

(S) Baggage Master __Tomor__   (U) Fireman __Larsen__

(V) Brakemen __McGarrigle__

(W) Train Crew went on duty __253pM__   (X) Must be relieved prior to __653a__

(Y) Engine Crew went on duty __203p__ M   (Z) Must be relieved prior to __1103a__

(AB) Individual members of train or engine crew excepted in above ordering and relieving time as follows:

__Tomor at 630 am up 1030 am__

__JOH 407 pme__

(I) Remarks. **This train was the eastbound section of the "Pennsylvania Limited" as it ran on the New York Division between between Broad Street and Penn Station**

F. Westing

___ Superintendent

The year 1914 saw the appearance of a new Pennsy Pacific. This one was a product of the drawing room of the Motive Power Department at Altoona, and was the work of James T. Wallis, General Superintendent of Motive Power. By then the running gear of the E6s of 1914 had been established as standard and a goodly part of it was appropriated by the new Pacific which bore a K4s classification. Fundamentally in cylinder and certain boiler sections it duplicated the K29s Pacific No. 3395, and like it together with many K2s and all the E6s class engines utilized the Alco screw reverse gear with its four-spoked dished handwheel.

Efficiencywise, measured on a power-to-weight basis, class K4s and the E6s were about equal. But the K4s had a much higher tractive force and a boiler of greater steaming capacity that provided for more sustained high speed running with heavier trains. It was, in fact, unmatched by any passenger type locomotive ever operated on the Pennsy until the first M1 dual service passenger and freight engine made its debut in 1923. This locomotive was of the Mountain, 4-8-2 type, and as previously noted used 72 inch drivers.

Another locomotive with 68 inch drivers of the 4-6-0 type known as class G5s came on the road also in 1923. With its 41,330 lb. tractive force, it proved a good performer in meeting its operating conditions, and in hilly terrain was at its best. Much work was done by these G5s engines in commuter traffic on the Pittsburgh Division and Schuylkill Division. Except for the one-window on each cab side and the shallow firebox, the boiler greatly resembled an E6s. Both the M1 and G5s have been plentifully illustrated elsewhere and scenes of these locomotives in action are available in profusion from photograph suppliers of railroadiana and books.

Getting back to the K4s Pacific, the first one was built in May 1914, No. 1737, at the Juniata Shops construction number 2825. For two years this engine was tested on the Altoona test plant and on the Pittsburgh Division, until 1917 when 41 new K4s class engines were built. While eminently suitable for the Pittsburgh Division they were scattered all over the Pennsy and were welcomed whole heartedly. Ultimately 425 units were built with 75 constructed by Baldwin, in 1927 at Eddystone, Pa. and the others at Juniata.

Originally the K4's had neat clean lines, a noted characteristic of Pennsy steam power in general. But toward the end of their days, and they lasted well into the diesel era, these cleancut lines were obliterated by the addition and relocation of certain details that in some degree were just superficial disfigurements without materially improving the locomotive's operation.

The eastbound Gotham Limited, train 54, as it passes around the Horseshoe Curve with a double-header of two K4s class locomotives in 1929. The first engine was No. 5072 formerly assigned to the Maryland Division. Tender on this engine was class 90P70, formerly 90F82 modified, as originally used on class I1s of the Decapod type. Changes included piping to permit steam heat to be fed to cars from locomotive, and a longer exposed slope sheet.

Engine No. 1413, class E2a built in 1902, at Juniata, wheels the southbound Congressional Limited through South Bristol, Pa., in September 1910. Trains then ran at street level in Bristol, but Pennsy was already working on track elevation through that city. This was completed and opened for service on Sunday, September 26, 1911. It shaved off about ¼-mile in length between New York and Philadelphia, and eliminated 12 grade crossings in Bristol. Cost of the project was $1,012,000.00. Signal bridge No. 682 was typical standard Pennsy design truss introduced in 1902 for main line use on New York Division, and later elsewhere east of Pittsburgh. The number 682 indicated that the bridge was 68.2 miles west of a fixed point in the Cortlandt Street Ferry Station, New York City, one mile east of the Jersey City Terminal across the Hudson River. Note pipe on right-side bridge support which was used to carry compressed air to signal mechanisms. This numbering of signal bridges made for quick location identification in the event of an emergency. Telephones were installed at these bridges to permit quick communication to the nearest interlocking tower. All signals were still of the lower quadrant automatic type and gave three indications per signal mast with two blades. Official Pennsy signal aspects characteristic of that period are included in this Chapter, and include lower and upper quadrant signal blade positions.

An eastbound K2 heads the Keystone Express train No. 20, as it passes around the wide curve adjoining the Crucible Steel Works at Harrison, New Jersey. Year was 1911. See how new and shiny those big Pacifics loomed up when compared with the smaller boilered Atlantics before the E6s 4-4-2's came on the scene. First car was a D70 class dining car.

Here we have a most interesting picture. It shows an E6s hauling the Pennsy's top-name train, No. 29, the Broadway Limited on August 11, 1917, after it had passed North Elizabeth station, N.J. Note how the safety valve is showing a white plume of steam, for those four Pullmans and one dining car were easy for that stubby barrel-chested Atlantic. Grand steamers those E6s engines, especially No. 460, the "Speed Queen" of the New York Division. Engine No. 460 is of exceptional interest and was the last E6s built at Juniata August 1914, construction number 2860. In this scene No. 460 was still equipped as in 1914 when new from Juniata Shops, oil headlight and all. No. 460 made the fastest time ever made by steam power between Washington, D.C., and Manhattan Transfer, N.J., on Sunday, June 11, 1927, when it hauled the Lindbergh Special. The 216 miles were covered in 175 minutes at an average speed of 74 mph. It was said that between Marcus Hook and Chester, Pa., No. 460 hit a speed of 115 mph., and was still not running on a wide-open throttle. I once had the great pleasure of driving a splendidly built live-steam model of engine No. 460, built to a 1-inch scale. We had a load of as I recall 7 adults and 8 children and the ease with which we started was remarkable. When we hit a grade a slight widening of the throttle caused the engine to speed up in a way that simulated jet propulsion— just like the prototype. Last but not least is the fact that this locomotive is still in existence at Strasburg, Pa., and will soon be enclosed in the State railroad museum at that location available for all who care to view it.

A westbound train heels to the curve at West Newark Junction in 1911 with a K2 at the head end while a busy fireman works on the fire.

Interior cab view of a K2 in 1911. Throttle lever is clearly visible, as is chain for opening and closing the firedoor. Handle of the reverse lever is directly underneath the throttle handle. Injector on right side was a Sellers, and that on the left was a Simplex. The former was manufactured by Sellers Company in Philadelphia, and the latter by Nathan Manufacturing Co. in New York City.

The first K2a class built at Juniata in 1911, construction number 2349. This class represented some slight changes from the K2 class, but the basic proportions were alike. Later, when superheated, these engines became class K2sa, and represented the most advanced design amongst the K2 category. Engineer Tom Towell of the New York Division had this engine assigned to him in the clocker service between New York and Philadelphia. His three sons all became Pennsy locomotive engineers on the New York Division. The tender on this locomotive had a high collar, but only carried it for about half the length of the tank. Very few of this half-collar tank were seen on the New York Division. On the road east of Pittsburgh, class K2 had their whistles located at an angle in back of the steam dome, as can be seen on No. 86.

Look how the big K2 on the right looms over the "big power" of an earlier day. The change in boiler size is the striking feature that distinguishes the giant Pacific No. 3357, from the Atlantic No. 5065, class E3sd, and the American No. 1655, class D13c.

Running on track No. 3, K2 class engine 3358 leaves Manhattan Transfer with a "clocker" in the summer of 1911. Jumpover Bridge No. 79 is the background and was used for the Hudson & Manhattan electric multiple-unit trains between 30 and 50 Church Street, New York and Park Place, Newark, N. J. It carried two tracks and the northbound track was used for a siding. When this picture was taken the H&M had not been completed to Newark, and shuttle service between Manhattan Transfer and Jersey City was made by steam trains. The tall-stacked locomotive at the right of the picture, probably a D14 class American type, was waiting to accommodate passengers for downtown New York on the next eastbound train.

Even a mighty K2 Pacific was glad to have the assistance of a little D16b when it climbed west with a heavy train around the Horseshoe Curve. Firemen are both working hard, as they usually did for the first uphill eleven miles out of Altoona with a westbound run.

A class K2a engine before superheating, but using a tender that was used more frequently on the road east of Pittsburgh. It was known as class 70P77, with a deck height of 77¼ inches from the rail top. This provided room for the stoker trough or conveyor in the event of equipping the locomotive with a stoker. Tender deck and cab floor were on the same level. These tenders were also known as "hopper tenders" for coal plates in the tank sloped downwards from the sides and back to the location where the stoker trough would be if ever applied. Due to this construction coal and water capacity approximated that of the low-sided 70P66 tanks despite its high collar. Engine 238 was built in 1911 at Juniata Shops, Altoona, Pa.

An engine of the E5 class built in 1910. Note the fabricated Kiesel trailing truck which appeared on this class before it was used on the first E6 locomotive built that same year.

Trains were still running to the big Jersey City train shed in 1910 when this picture was taken. The two wooden Parlor cars at the head end, plus the following all-steel P70 class coaches tell the story. For with the opening of Penn Station in New York on November 27th, 1910, wooden passenger carrying equipment was forbidden. Engine 3148, class E2d, and one of 25 such locomotives built at Juniata in 1906, is, with a clear stack, speedily hauling this eastbound Clocker somewhere between Eddington and Croydon, Pa.

Two Pittsburgh Division engines of the E3a class hauling a heavy westbound train are working hard as they climb the grade leading to the Horseshoe Curve.

A cold winter day finds two light Atlantics climbing the Narberth grade with a westbound train having a mixed consist of two wooden baggage cars and all-steel passenger rolling stock.

Engine No. 318 on the Altoona test plant that was designed by Axel Vogt. This locomotive was built in May, 1908, as class E3d, but as shown here after it had become class E3sd. It still retained the spoked forward truck wheels, and three piece cylinder and saddle construction. The object of this latter arrangement was to enable more rapid replacement of a cylinder and valve in the event of damage. The Vogt vacuum relief valve is enclosed in a casing on top of the valve chest. This locomotive produced more power per pound of weight than any passenger locomotive tested including the first K4s Pacific built years later. Engine 318 developed one cylinder horsepower for every 94.6 pounds of weight. But it was the superheater that gave this locomotive its outstanding mark of distinction, for it permitted an increase of 14 per cent in drawbar pull at 20 mph, and 39 per cent at 50 mph. Superheater damper counterweight is in "down" position as it should be when the throttle is shut. The driving wheels rested upon blind tires of 72 inch diameter supporting wheels to which were fastened Alden absorption brakes. These offered hydraulic resistance to the driving wheels, thereby absorbing the power developed by the locomotive and by causing the engine to overcome this resistance it was possible to obtain the actual tractive force and drawbar pull characteristics which were measured by a traction dynamometer in a small building in back of the locomotive. Engineer Martin Lee often drove this locomotive and commented "Superheater works fine." He had driven 318 when it used saturated steam and could readily spot the improvement. No. 318 was later renumbered 4098, and taken out of service in 1937.

Besides getting bigger power with the K2 Pacifics, the Pennsy began to beef up their smaller passenger engines such as the light Atlantics and D16b Americans. This was done by the application of a superheater and enlarged cylinders. Locomotives with a good life expectancy were thus brought to a condition where they conformed to the latest design of a specific class. As a typical example, engine 3159 is shown here at the Meadows enginehouse in June 1913. Its cylinder diameter was widened, superheater applied, and outside steam pipes fed steam to the valve chests. Solid disc wheels replaced the former spoked wheels in the forward truck. With these changes engine 3159, a former class E2d built in 1906, matched the latest E3sd class engine of that day in power and performance. Another addition was a brick arch supported on water tubes in the firebox, that aided greatly in smoke reduction. The tender, however was that used on the earlier Atlantics going back to 1901.

The northbound Congressional Limited, train No. 60, gracefully swings around a curve in Maryland with an E3d engine 5127, built in 1907, at the head end. Date was 1912, and regular daily train consist in following order from the engine was as follows:

    1 Parlor-Baggage Car
    1 Dining Car
    4 Parlor Cars
    1 Parlor-Observation Car

This seven car make-up differed from the southbound section of this train in that it had an extra Parlor Car, but omitted the Railway Post Office (RPO) car then class M-70. All the cars were Pullmans except the Dining Car which was owned and operated by the Pennsy. Cars were of all-steel construction and Pullmans had sheathed metal sides that simulated wooden tongue and groove boards. Many travelers, doubt it or not, in those days, believed that they would be electrocuted if the train were struck by lightning when riding in a steel car. As a concession Pullman "faked" the steel sheathing to allay their apprehensions. The Congressional Limited left Washington, D.C., at 4 p.m. and arrived at Penn Station, New York at 9 p.m. Both northbound and southbound sections of this train took five hours to complete the trip, though even then it could have been made in much less time. At Manhattan Transfer 8.8 miles from Penn Station, steam power was swapped for electric and a DD-1 motor hauled the train over the Jersey Meadows, under Weehawken and the Hudson River to the Pennsy's monumental gateway to the west and south. From there it went to Sunnyside yards in Long Island City, where it was made ready for its southbound trip on the following day.

Engine No. 10 as it looked in the 1930's, with split saddle cylinders and valves, changed arrangement of outside steam pipes, new cab and roof ventilator, round-cased headlight and steam turbine-electric generator. Air piping has been rearranged and train control equipment under the smokebox added to provide duplication of wayside signals in the cab. This locomotive at the time was used regularly in the Jersey City-New Brunswick passenger service. It continued in this service until the coming of electrification when MU trains took over the work so ably handled by old No. 10.

Light Atlantics were still in evidence in 1912 and for years after despite the use of K2 class Pacifics. On comparatively level divisions they could make the schedule and were often used on the New York-Washington runs. Here we see E3d class engine No. 917 built in 1908, southbound with train No. 95, the Atlantic Coast Line Express made up of eight all-steel cars. Another reason for frequently using the light Atlantics was to "run out" their revenue mileage and thus justify the initial investment per locomotive. For by then more K2 class engines were in use and the even larger K4s Pacifics were anticipated. In fact, in 1917, 41 engines of the K4s class came on the road, and in 1918, 111 more made their appearance. Quite a few immediately went into the New York-Washington, New York-Harrisburg service; even "clockers" between New York and Philadelphia occasionally got one. Due to this there was an unusually large amount of these light Atlantics working runs between New York and Washington in 1916, and frequently doubleheaded if the load was exceptionally heavy. Note how accurately the telegraph poles fall in line alongside the tangent section of track. Looks like one pole with a multiplicity of crossarms; good surveying and pole plumbing, that!

Modernization of the light Atlantics on Lines West differed from that used east of Pittsburgh. While sub-classes E2, E2a, E2b, and E2c, were fitted with superheaters and otherwise changed to conform with latest light Atlantics elsewhere, they varied in some respects. This can be seen on former class E2b engine No. 7484 built at Juniata in 1906. Valve chests and piston valves were placed on top of the cylinders, and outside steam pipes fed superheated steam to them in a more direct manner than formerly. A new two-part split saddle cylinder replaced the older arrangement, but inside Stephenson valvegear was retained. Other changes are apparent, and in this new guise No. 7484 became class E7s. Class E2 on Lines West with its radial-stay firebox was similarly revamped, but was given an E7sa designation. This distinguished it from the light Atlantics using Belpaire fireboxes such as classes E2a, E2b, and E2c. None of the light Atlantics west of Pittsburgh appear to have ever used the Walschaerts valve gear.

A round-top firebox Atlantic speeds by North Elizabeth in 1913 with a New York bound Clocker. Engine is No. 837 and was built at Juniata in 1901. Most likely it then sported a single combination dome and sandbox, but later they were separated as shown.

Many have seen the right side of this locomotive, the forty-thousandth locomotive built by Baldwin, but the left side has been neglected, so here it is. Note the beautiful lettering and striping all in genuine gold leaf per standard Pennsy practice. Engine No. 8661 was fired by a Crawford mechanical stoker, and its driving steam cylinder can be seen under the bottom of the cab. Reciprocating action of the piston to operate the stoker was made by admission of steam to a Westinghouse reversing valve as used on their standard 9½ inch air compressors. The Crawford stoker was of the underfeed type wherein coal was fed upwardly into retorts or troughs and into the firebox. This caused the coal to be ''coked'' to a great extent, thereby, cutting down greatly on smoke and noxious gases. This particular engine of class K3s which had 26 × 26 inch cylinders, was assigned to the Pan Handle line of the Pennsy between Pittsburgh and St. Louis.

Last of two additional superheated pilot models of ''The Big E'' was No. 1092 which due to its novel valve gear became class E6sa. Up to 1923 the letter ''s'' indicated the use of a superheater on Pennsy locomotives used in road power. One exception was an experimental Mountain type engine class M1. Engine 1092 was built in June 1912, just after engine No. 89, which was the first of the E6 group built with a superheater, making it the first E6s. The valve gear on No. 1092 was the invention of Otis W. Young of Chicago, Illinois, and was known as the Young-Mann-Averill gear. It used rotary valves, and was driven by Walschaerts motion as shown in this illustration. The Young gear was soon removed and replaced with the standard Pennsy arrangement of the Walschaerts gear, and became class E6s.

Engine No. 1179 of the E6s class on the ready track at the Meadows, N. J., in 1914. The earlier E6s engines built in 1914 had sandboxes similar to those used on engine No. 1092. The clean-cut lines, and well proportioned details are strikingly evident. This was the Pennsy's pride and most powerful Atlantic type locomotive ever built at the time. This was one of 80 E6s engines built in 1914, these and the three that preceded them made a total of 83 super-powerful Atlantics. All three pilot engines, were later changed to conform to the engine seen here. Some, however still kept the old style sandbox. A complete story of these engines can be found in the author's APEX OF THE ATLANTICS, published by Kalmbach Pub. Co. Milwaukee, Wis. 53233.

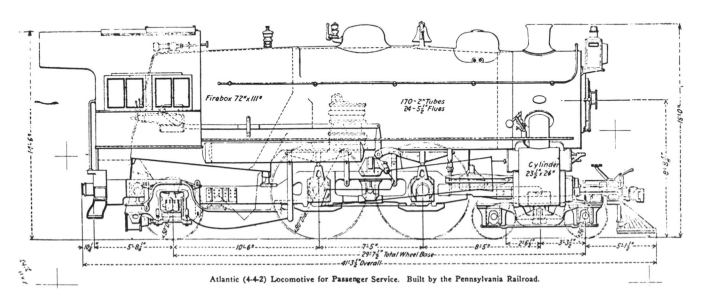

Atlantic (4-4-2) Locomotive for Passenger Service. Built by the Pennsylvania Railroad.

Diagram of the E6s of 1914 Front pilot beam has been replaced by a step. But I never saw an E6s or even a picture of one that had a dome whistle from 1912 on.

An E6s at the water plug in Atlantic City, N.J. No. 6028 hauled many high-speed express trains between Atlantic City, Camden, Philadelphia and New York.

Engine 782, class E6s many years after 1914, at 40th Street Yard in West Philadelphia. Many changes readily apparent have been made since the day this engine emerged from the Juniata Erecting Shop. Some were made by the Pennsy on their own initiative, but I.C.C. regulations accounted for some other changes.

A doubleheader near Radnor, Pa., in 1911. Leading engine is No. 2427, class E3a built 1903. Many Atlantics were used singly and in tandem at this time and for some years afterwards on heavy and lighter trains in order to run out their revenue mileage, and thereby, amortize their investment value. This happened quite frequently despite the availability of K2 and E6s engines. I recall that many light Atlantics doubleheaded trains between Manhattan Transfer and Washington in 1916.

A K2s takes water at high speed from the trank tanks at Radnor, Pa.

Class K2sa engine built at Juniata for Pennsylvania Lines at Fort Wayne, Indiana in 1916. The use of two 9½ inch air compressors was a regular thing on Lines West big power at that time rather than one 8½ cross-compound pump. Slight deviations from K2 class engines east of Pittsburgh can be seen in the grab iron encircling the front end of the smokebox, the steps on the smokebox braces, and whistle location. Under the cab is the steam cylinder of the Crawford mechanical stoker. The tender was arranged for stoker firing and had a deck that was level with the cab floor. Class of tender was 70P77a, originally Lines West class 6A. Distance between truck centers was 14 feet 8 inches. Lines West K2's had the safety valves located on the roof sheet of the firebox, usually enclosed in an auxiliary dome, though sometimes exposed. Later all K2 Pacifics had their safety valves arranged in a similar fashion. Torch for night inspection can be seen in back of cab door.

The northbound Congressional Limited in 1916 speeding through the Maryland countryside on its run to New York. Unlike the southbound run the Railway Post Office (RPO) car was omitted, but an extra Parlor Car brought the consist up to the normal seven-car train. Engine is a class E3sd and has had its 9½ inch donkey pump replaced by an 8½ inch cross-compound air compressor. Piping from turret leading to the smokebox was part of the Wyman drifting valve. This device gave automatic action when the engine was drifting by preventing a vacuum and, thereby, blocking an intake of cinders and carbonization of lubricating oil in the cylinders. It was the patented invention of George W. Wyman, of the PWB&W RR at Wilmington, Del. Wyman's drifting valve was also applied to an engine of the D16sb, H9s, and K2sa classes.

Lending a helping hand to a light Atlantic with a heavy train, a K2 passes a bracket post signal on the Philadelphia Division. Scene shows train somewhere east of Paoli. After 1916 this part of the Pennsy between Broad Street Station and Paoli, Pa. became part of the Philadelphia Terminal Division.

A New York Division fireman on an eastbound "clocker" stands alongside K2s engine 3356 at North Philadelphia Station in 1921. This was the only superheated K2 that I ever saw on this division that omitted outside steam pipes to the valve chests. It also retained its sandbox location behind the bell as originally placed until scrapped in January 1933.

A K2sa engine No. 1350 built in 1913, heads a speedy late afternoon express from Philadelphia bound for Atlantic City in 1928. It is shown leaving North Philadelphia, and I recall the first car was a wooden Parlor car named Laurette, painted Pullman green.

Even in the late 1920's after the K4s class had taken over the job of hauling the top-name trains the K2s class still hauled the best. Here engine No. 1458 a New York Division K2s built in 1910 heads the westbound St. Louisan, then the Pennsy's best on the New York-St. Louis run, and made up of solid Pullman stock, a first-class train in every respect. This engine like 3356 also had its sandbox in back of the bell and, as originally built dropped sand on the middle drivers only. This arrangement also lasted until the locomotive was scrapped many years later.

Flat side view of the first K4s class locomotive. It was built in May 1914, and numbered 1737. Tender was class 70P70, which was later used on many E6s Atlantics. The casing outside the cab housed part of the screw reverse gear mechanism which enabled the cab to be shortened considerably. Chassis was similar to that of the 1914 E6s engines, but later, changes were made on this engine and following K4s Pacifics in the spring equalization system at the front end. Two coil springs were in time placed under each axle box of the trailing truck, and materially improved its riding quality. This truck, the famed "KW" type was a direct appropriation from the E6s.

One of the only two K2sb engines heads a New York-Washington express not far from Union Station. Still in fine fettle, although built in 1911. No. 3371 stood up to speedy service requirements most satisfactorily despite its 72 inch drivers. The application of a better trailing truck—KW type—and cab signals, indicates that they expected the old girl to hang around quite awhile. Still retained, however, was the wooden pilot beam made of white oak 12 × 12 inches thick and around 9 feet in length. Train engine was a K2sa No. 5014. Many K2s engines were around until complete electrification of the New York Division, and for some time on non-electrified lines of the Pennsy and Long Island Railroad.

Engineer Ed Vaughn with K4s engine 2445 heads the south-bound Congressional Limited past North Elizabeth, N.J., on June 5, 1921. Wooden pilot had given way to the metal slatted, or "hen coop" pattern. Small pipe from the steam dome fed steam to the turbine-electric generator set to power the complete locomotive and tender lighting equipment. Later, this small pipe was placed underneath the outside boiler jacket thus eliminating the unsightly look of the exposed pipe.

Heading the southbound Congressional Limited on July 8, 1919, at North Elizabeth, N.J., is K4s engine 3670, with Archie Nizer at the throttle.

One of the early K4s engines built in 1917 at Juniata. Still using an oil-burning headlight, and wooden pilot, the engine stands on the "ready track" about to start for Manhattan Transfer where it will pick up its train for Washington, D.C. The 8½ inch cross-compound air compressor was fed steam from the steam dome instead of from a steam turret inside the cab as was done on the first K4s No. 1737. The piping on this engine No. 5022 showing this arrangement can plainly be seen. A 1-inch pipe in back of the stack was known as a smoke lifter, but around 1925 its use began to be discontinued. Engine 5022 was assigned to the Maryland Division.

A new K4s of the early days heads the seven-car Congressional Limited bound for New York at Halethorpe, Maryland.

Another view of No. 1737 taken at Altoona in 1914. Wooden pilot and metal pilot beam duplicate those used on the E6s engines of 1914.

Engine 3678 built in 1918 at Juniata and of the K4s class, heads the eastbound Broadway Limited at high speed on the Metuchen, N.J., curve. From a short distance west of this point an experienced fireman could ride the seatbox all the way to Manhattan Transfer for about 18 miles. Picture was taken shortly after 1923, and a typical train consist of this train could well have been as follows:

M70	6546 (R.P.O. car)	Engine 3678, class K4s
PLB	West Willow	All cars painted tuscan red
SL	Domingo	
SL	Antiphon	
DN	7958	
SL	Euripides	
SL	St. Davids	
OBS-SL	Brookview	

Another rare Pennsy scene showing the big Alco Pacific class K29s locomotive in action. It was assisting a K4s class engine in getting a heavy westbound express train moving uphill to Gallitzin at the crest of the grade. Train is a few miles west of Altoona, Pa., and passengers may soon be able to see the powerful doubleheader as the train rolls around the scenic Horseshoe Curve. Note the offset location of the bell on No. 3395, the K29s class engine, and the forward position of the two single-stage air compressors. The 3395 had one main air reservoir placed between the main frames out of sight. This aided its cleancut appearance but did not make things easier for the locomotive inspectors at the enginehouse.

The eastbound Broadway Limited approaching Morrisville station in 1925. Heading the train is engine 5373 built at Juniata Shops in 1924. Tender is class 70P70d, and engine and tender represented the most recent development of class K4s at the time. First car was a class M70 United States Mail, Railway Post Office car. On Sundays the Broadway did not have a mail car in the train's consist when it departed from New York and Chicago.

Interior of cab view of a K4s showing how they looked in the 1920's and early 1930's. Firedoor was still hand opened as can be seen by door-opening chain. This backhead first came into use on the 3700 series of fifty K4s engines built in 1920. Reversing screw handwheel was used, and there were four gauges, one marked "Locomotive" which recorded the boiler pressure, one marked "Steam" to denote pressure of steam heat going to train, and two air brake gauges. Outside injectors of the non-lifting type have their check valves right and left in the cab to which are connected the curved delivery pipes. The left-side check valve has the squirt hose valve connected to it, and above it is the sight-feed lubricator with pipes feeding to various parts of the locomotive. Man on right side of cab has right hand on throttle lever and left hand on automatic brake valve. Curves in delivery pipes served two purposes; they provided expansion bends and cleared the grab iron above the oil can and night torch tray above the firedoor.

A picture I well recall, for I took it on my birthday July 17, 1926, from the Spring Garden Street bridge. It shows the westbound Pennsylvania Limited, train No. 5, passing through West Phila-delphia, with a train of twelve cars. It was the year of the Sequi-Centennial celebration, and travel was heavy especially on a Saturday with many passengers coming and going. Consequently additional cars were added to this train which was all Pullman and extra fare. First two cars were painted Pullman green and the rest tuscan red. The parlor-baggage car coupled to the tender was named Eagle Springs. The Limited had just left West Philadelphia Station, and was beginning the 21 mile climb to Paoli. The blasting exhaust of the engine was deafening! Locomotive was K4s class No. 3807 built at Juniata in 1923 and assigned to the Philadelphia Division. Turret casing normally in front of the cab roof atop the firebox roof sheet was missing that day, and steam valves feeding the outside injector steam pipes as well as other valves were exposed. The tender was known as class 90P70 with two four-wheel trucks and 36 inch wheels. This design of tank had originally been used on the Pennsy's I1s class Decapods then class 90F82. With some changes it was converted to passenger locomotive use. Its high tank collar was a predominant feature making more room for additional coal and water. Up to the appearance of the Kiesel tender which came out this same year of 1926, class 90P70 represented the latest in K4s tenders regarding capacity. As the engine passed by I saw that the engineer was standing up adjusting the storm window in front of the cab. Look at that load of coal in the tender and pity the poor fireman on this hot summer day on a hand-fired job as 3807 was in those days. The Pennsylvania Limited was still running via Broad Street Station in Philadelphia with the consist of cars reversed over the New York Division. On this day two Pennsy dining cars were coupled together in this train adding 180 tons to the ten Pullmans in tow. Schedule allowed two hours for the 105 mile run to Harrisburg where a Middle Division engine took over. Up to its last shopping engine 3807 had covered 1,972,000 miles.

The eastbound Broadway Limited, train 28, hauled by K4s engine 5396 in May 1927. Tender was class 70-P70d. The cars are still on the five-tracked stone arch bridge as they cross the Schuylkill River.

Engine 3750 with 17 cars in tow, all heavyweight Pullmans. The big K4s was probably hauling a night train from New York and omitted dining car service. It was speedily approaching the Washington Union Station. The locomotive itself is of interest, as it hauled President Harding's funeral train, and now with its number changed to 1737 reposes at Strasburg, Pa.

As an engineer told me, "The 3700's were sharp engines" and here we see No. 3738 hauling the "Spirit of St. Louis" between South Elizabeth and Linden, N. J. in the rain. Train No. 31 was as odd number indicates headed for the west, and was running on track No. 4. The Pennsy had six main-line tracks—still does—between South Elizabeth and Rahway, N.J.

Engine 3877 sports the new Kiesel tender patented by William F. Kiesel, the Mechanical Engineer who succeeded Axel Vogt.

K4s engine built in 1920 when the whole lot of fifty were turned out at Altoona, heads a New York bound, Florida East Coast Express.''

A Baldwin built K4s ready to leave Broad Street Station, Philadelphia. When new from the builder a round number plate was located on the smokebox front. The sandbox grabiron on each side of the sandbox, stirrup-step under the cab and grabiron above were omitted. Engine 5404 was for some time frequently used on both the west and eastbound Broadway Limited.

The Pennsylvania Limited westbound between South Elizabeth, and Linden, N.J., headed by a Baldwin K4s No. 5409. This engine was regularly assigned to train No. 5, and I often saw it in action on this train. By this time the Limited had lost its "all Pullman" status, and had a day coach in its consist. It also ran via the New York-Pittsburgh subway tunnel in West Philadelphia, thereby, bypassing Broad Street and West Philadelphia Stations.

In 1927 the Pennsy ordered 100 new K4s class locomotives with Kiesel tenders, class 110P70. These engines were numbered 5400 to 5499. It was the first time an order for this class was given to an outside builder. Baldwin got the order to construct 75 of these locomotives, Nos. 5400 to 5474, and Altoona built the remaining 25, Nos. 5475 to 5499. They represented exceptionally high power for hand-fired engines, and were generally similar in details to the K4s engines built in 1923 and 1924, which represented the latest development of this class up to 1927. But the basic specifications of boiler, cylinders, drivers and boiler pressure remained the same as on No. 1737 built in 1914. The last five built at Altoona Nos. 5495 to 5499, had the main frames, cross braces, cylinders and valve chests, embodied in one integral or frame-bed casting. All these big Pacifics had Alco power reverse gears and compressed air provided the muscle for reversing and "notching up" at speed. The smoke lifter and its pipe in back of the stack was dispensed with, and a sturdier form of guide and crosshead was used. A greater cutting away of the cab roof overhang was made as can be seen right above the canvas storm curtain in back of the cab window. With the inclusion of this last group of K4s engines ever built for the Pennsy, they had acquired 425 engines of this one class. This represented more Pacific type locomotives ever owned by any American railroad. With passing years previously built engines of this class were rebuilt to conform to the 1927 engines. Subsequent changes such as front-end throttles, improved exhaust nozzles, and the use of stokers with larger tenders, and new locations for the turbine electric-generator and headlight became part of the K4s engines in their last days. Cast-steel pilots and new locations for the automatic cab signal control equipment also were a part of these latter day modifications.

A Baldwin K4s No. 5406, heads the Crescent Limited at Moore, Pa. in 1929, on the Maryland Division. This train with its Pullmans painted in "Southern Green" was a most colorful sight. This section of the division had been electrified between Philadelphia and Wilmington in September 1928. This accounts for the catenary system above the train and the tubular poles that supported the high-tension transmission lines. Engine 5406 was still hand-fired, and the original 110-P-70 class Kiesel tenders were coupled to the 100 engines of this group, namely, 5400 to 5499.

Here we have an authentic dining car menu used on the Pennsylvania Limited one day in the 1920's. Those appetizing specialties and the prices that go with them would be heartily welcomed today.

The name of your waiter is

LOGAN MARTIN

THE PENNSYLVANIA LIMITED

LUNCHEON

SOUPS—
Cream of Leeks, Princesse, Tureen 45; Cup 30
Clam Bouillon, Hot or Cold 30
Clear Green Turtle 50
Consomme, Brunoise, Tureen 45; Cup 30

RELISHES—
Ripe, Green or Stuffed Olives 25   Stuffed Mangoes 30   Celery 35
Sauerkraut Juice 25   Tomato Juice 25

OYSTERS AND FISH—
Oysters (6) on Half Shell 40; Cocktail 50; Fried, Tartar Sauce 80
Stewed in Cream 75   Stewed in Milk 60
Filets of Sole, Remoulade, Hashed Browned Potatoes 95
Broiled Fresh Mackerel, Hoteliere, Julienne Potatoes 95
Creamed Finnan Haddie with Green Peppers 65

SPECIALTIES—
Grilled Combination with French Fried Potatoes
(Lamb Chop, Sausage, Bacon, Tomato) 1.25
Spring Chicken, Maryland Style 1.25
Devilled Roast Beef with Hashed Browned Potatoes 1.10
Cold Roast Leg of Lamb, Mint Jelly, String Bean Salad 1.10
Omelet with Oysters, Poulette, Glazed Sweet Potatoes 1.00
Vegetarian Luncheon with Poached Egg 95

GRILLED—
Lamb Chop 65   Sirloin Steak 1.75   Young Chicken (Half) 1.25
Minute Steak, French Fried or Hashed Browned Potatoes 1.25
Ham and (2) Eggs 80
Bacon and (2) Eggs 80
Ham 80; Half Portion 45
Bacon 80; Half Portion 45; per Slice 15

EGGS AND OMELETS—
Eggs—Boiled, Fried, Shirred or Scrambled (1) 30; (2) 40
Poached (2) on Toast 50
Omelets, (3) Eggs, Plain 60; Ham, Parsley or Jelly 70
Omelet with Stewed Fresh Cranberries 75

COLD MEATS, ETC.—
Ham 85   Ox Tongue 90   Sliced Chicken 1.25
Roast Beef 1.00   Assorted Cold Meats 1.25
Potato Salad Served with Cold Meats
Frankfurters (Hot or Cold) with Potato Salad 85
Baked Beans 45   Sardines 65

VEGETABLES—
Beets in Butter 30   New Carrots, Saute 30
Stewed Tomatoes 30   New String Beans 40
New Peas 40   Fresh Spinach 35; with Egg 45
Potatoes:-   Boiled 25   Mashed 30
French Fried 35   Hashed Browned 35
Hashed in Cream 35   Glazed Sweet 35

SANDWICHES—
Fried Ham 45   Fried Egg 35   Fried Ham and Egg 55
Ham 30   Cheese 30   Chicken 50
Cold Roast Beef 50   Tongue 30

SALADS with Saltine Wafers—
Apple and Celery, Mayonnaise 65
Head Lettuce; French, Mayonnaise or Thousand Island Dressing 40;
with Tomato 50
Combination 60; with Roquefort or Pennsylvania Dressing 25 cents extra
Pineapple, French Dressing 55   Chicken 1.00
Asparagus, Vinaigrette 50   Potato 40

BREAD, ETC.—
Vienna, Raisin, Graham or Rye 15   Muffins (2) 15   Rolls 15
Crackers 10   Whole Wheat Wafers 15
Dry or Buttered Toast 20   Bran Cookies 15   Boston Brown 15
Doughnuts (2) 15   Raisin Bread, Toasted 20

DESSERTS—
Apple Pie 25; with Cheese 35
Deep Dish Berry Pie (Baked on Car To-day) 30
Baked Apple with Cream 35   Raw Apple 15
Stewed Fresh Cranberries 25
Grape Fruit 35   Chilled Casaba Melon 40
French Ice Cream 35   Wafers 15
Preserved Figs in Syrup 50   Preserved Strawberries 35
Orange Marmalade 35   Bar le Duc 35
Hawaiian Pineapple 35   Guava Jelly 30
Wine Jellies 25   Orange 20

CHEESE AND CRACKERS—
Swiss Gruyere 35   Imperial 30   Cream 30
Roquefort 40   Yeast Cake 10

TEA, COFFEE, ETC.—
Orange Pekoe, India, English Breakfast, or Oolong Tea (Pot for One) 25
Coffee (Pot for One) 25   (Demitasse) 15   Postum 30
Cocoa (Pot for One) 30   Iced Tea Coffee or Cocoa (Pot for One) 30
Kaffee Hag or Sanka Coffee (Pot for One) 35
Certified Milk (Individual Bottle) 20   Malted Milk 30
Service charge of twenty-five cents will be made
for each person served outside of Dining Car.
*Pay only upon presentation of check; see that
extensions and totals are correct.*

Passengers are requested to report any unusual service or attention on the part of employees. This enables us to recognize the exceptional efficiency which we wish to encourage in our service.
F. W. Conner, Passenger Traffic Manager, Philadelphia, Pa.
C. E. Milliron, Superintendent, Dining Car Service, New York, N. Y.

.... B. J. THOMAS, Steward in Charge

Chapter 8
Freight Trains (1890's to 1920's)

Unquestionably, the greatest revenue producer on American railroads to this day is freight traffic. Consequently, on railroads where freight was the major commodity of traffic, locomotives built for this service predominated. There were some exceptions such as the Long Island Rail Road, the former West Jersey & Seashore Railroad, and the defunct New York Westchester & Boston Railway. But those roads were electrified and the bulk of their traffic was operated by multiple-unit cars.

The Pennsy, touching as it did, so many States with vast potentials for freight business was well provided with freight locomotives to move such traffic in voluminous quantity expeditiously. Though less spectacular than the graceful light Atlantics, or trim American type, in point of speed and elegance of their train consists, these freight engines were the moneymaking workhorses that helped the Pennsy mightily in turning dreams into reality, such as Penn Station in New York City, and scores of other vital projects imperative to progressive railroad operation.

While the Pennsy employed Moguls, class F, of the 2-6-0 type, and 4-6-0 type ten-wheelers, class G, both with various sub-classifications, it was the plodding 2-8-0 type Consolidations, class H, (old classes I and R) that did the most in moving the mountainous tonnage that rolled unceasingly over the Pennsy between the 1890's and the 1920's. This was particularly the case on the road east of Pittsburgh, where classes H6, H8, and H9, with their numerous sub-classes, and ear-piercing short-belled screech-tone whistles, did their part in keeping the wheels of commerce moving.

Up until 1916, the Pennsy was having Consolidations built, and they worked for many years before retirement. On the road east of Pittsburgh class H9s represented the largest in weight and tractive force, while on Lines West, class H10s with larger cylinders was the peak of Pennsy Consols.

As we have seen in the preceding Chapter, class H8 introduced in 1907, not only set the pattern for these massive 2-8-0's, but also played a big part in the creation of the E6s class Atlantics, the like of which had never been seen before.

To show what these early H8 locomotives could do even before superheating, the following record is presented. Let us look at some of the work these big Consolidations did on the Middle Division back in 1909.

By far the heaviest freight train ever hauled by one locomotive at the time, on any railroad in America, and probably in the world, was hauled over the Pennsylvania Railroad, between Altoona and Enola, near Harrisburg, Pa., (127 miles) by a single locomotive No. 1113, on June 22, 1909, in 7 hours and 12 minutes, at an average speed of 17.6 mph. The train consisted of 105 steel cars loaded with 5,544 tons of coal.

This record was the culmination of a series of tests made for the purpose of determining the hauling power of the most improved types of locomotives used in the regular freight service of the Pennsy over the grades of the Middle Division. The latest link in a chain of improvements in this area resulted in grade reduction and removal of curvature that had been completed and opened to service shortly before between Mount Union and Ryde.

Locomotive No. 1113, which hauled this train was built at Juniata in 1908, and known as class H8b. It developed a tractive force of 45,327 pounds. Each car carried more than 105,600 pounds of coal in each car of this train, which gave a total weight of coal alone over 11,000,000 pounds. The entire train, including engine and caboose and cars weighed 7,644 tons or 15,288,000 pounds. The length of this train was 3600 feet, more than two-thirds of a mile.

The best previous record of a heavy freight movement on the Middle Division, was made on June 18th, 1909, when a train of 94 steel cars, loaded with coal, and weighing 13,844,000 pounds, made the run between Altoona and Enola in 7 hours and 31 minutes.

Other runs made during the month of June 1909, which exceeded in train weight any previous records, were as follows:

for the Pacific type on the Pennsy, and his firm support for the Consols and Atlantics, spurred Alfred W. Gibbs to his best efforts in the development of the brutish 2-8-0's and later, the classic E6s Atlantics. Other roads had long gone from these two types to the ten-wheelers, Prairies, Pacifics, Mountain type, Mikados, Decapods, and the 2-10-2 type Santa Fe's, but not the Pennsy—as yet!

By 1914 Mr. Ely was no longer with the Pennsy, and Alfred Gibbs had been sent to Philadelphia as a Consultant regarding motive power, rather than holding the more authoritative position he had at Altoona. A new man, but a good one, then held the reins at Altoona, one James T. Wallis. He was ably supported, as was Gibbs, by Axel Vogt, Mechanical Engineer, and William F. Kiesel, Jr., Assistant Mechanical Engineer. Wallis from the start set about further improving Pennsy steam power, and the year 1914 saw something outstanding in the road's motive power history. And that was the use of an identical boiler suitable for either their new K4s Pacific, or slightly newer Mikado. This was the first time that such an inter-changeable boiler had been built for Pennsy locomotives suitable for freight and passenger engines. In 1913 the Pennsy was evincing an interest in the Mikado

Date	Engine (1) Number	Class	Date Built	Number of Cars	Total Weight of Train (3)	Time Hrs.	Min.
June 3	3212	H8	1907	85 Mixed (2)	4852 tons	12	30
June 5	1641	H8b	1908	86 Mixed	4922	9	42
June 8	2905	H8b	1908	87 Mixed	4623	10	21
June 8	451	H8b	1908	75 Steel	5348	10	12
June 8	2903	H8b	1908	75 Steel	5348	8	2
June 8	3212	H8	1907	75 Steel	5307	10	21
June 14	1113	H8b	1908	85 Steel	6151	7	15

(1) All locomotives were built by Penna. RR. at Juniata Shops, Altoona, Pa.
(2) In this instance "Mixed" meant a train of wooden and steel cars, as compared to an all-steel freight car consist.
(3) Includes engine, weight of cars, their contents and caboose.

Not long after though, another class H8b engine No. 1221, built at Juniata in 1909, ran from Altoona to Enola with 120 steel cars loaded with coal and a train weight of 8850 tons. The run was made in 6 hours and 29 minutes, making an average speed of 20 mph.

As enjoined by the Biblical injunction, the Pennsy believed in "Holding fast to that which is true." This attitude accounted for their high regard for Consolidations in freight service, and four-coupled locomotives (Americans and Atlantics) in passenger train operation. Mr. T. N. Ely, Pennsy motive power Chief, was not known for his enthusiasm

2-8-2 type locomotive, and a trial Mikado, No. 1752 was built at Juniata in April 1914. Known as class L1s, the railroaders soon dubbed them "lollipops" and from 1914 and several years after Juniata and Baldwin turned them out in large quantity.

Tests on the Altoona plant showed that the L1s gave an increase of 25 per cent in maximum tractive force with a weight increase of 30 per cent. The Consolidations were clearly outmoded, as the "Mikes" by producing higher steaming capacity in proportion to their adhesion proved themselves speedier engines with heavier trains than the H9s Consolidations. Still, the Consols were active at certain points on the Pennsy and paid for their monetary investment many times over before leaving the scene.

Like the H9s class Consols built in 1913, the cylinders, valve chambers, and saddle were cast in two halves. Outside steam pipes fed really hot superheated steam directly to the valves as this served to prevent excessive expansion or contraction in the cylinder saddle which might occur with highly superheated steam passing through it.

With 1916 came a brutish Juniata built class Ils Decapod 2-10-0 type locomotive No. 790, that featured a half-stroke or limited cut-off when the locomotive was operating in full gear. Motivation behind the design was the fact that steam locomotives were frequently operated beyond the point of economical working. Especially was this so with helper locomotives which ran almost steadily with a cut-off near the end of the stroke. Altoona thereupon concluded if they could design a locomotive to operate at 50 per cent cut-off in full gear, without sacrificing drawbar pull, they would gain the difference between coal and water rates at full stroke and those at half-stroke, or about 25 per cent.

With a cut-off of 50 per cent in full gear it became necessary to use enlarged cylinders and a higher boiler pressure to develop tractive force in proportion to adhesion when only admitting steam for half-stroke in full gear. This was accomplished by using cylinders 30½ × 32 inches, combined with a boiler pressure of 250 pounds. Fixing the cut-off at a figure of 50 per cent when in full gear was obtained by

merely increasing the steam lap of the valves 2 inches. And then, to meet the requirements of starting an auxiliary port was cut in the valve cages 1¾ inches in advance of each of the main steam ports. These ports were intended for starting, but were, however, in action at all times when the engine was using steam. They were ⅛ inch by 1½ inch and were so located that the valve had a steam lap of ¼ inch. This exceedingly small port, while quite sufficient to build up pressure in the cylinder equal to that in the boiler in a very short time when the engine was standing, was so small and admitted such small quantities of steam that it produced no appreciable effect when the piston was in motion, and its influence could not be detected on the indicator cards.

Built mainly for freight drag-speed service and bucking the hilly terrain of the Pittsburgh Division, nonetheless, speeds of 50 mph were obtained from these "hippos" as they came to be known. Test plant and road tests demonstrated that these engines compared with the L1s Mikados, showed a power increase of 41 per cent over the 2-8-2's, with a decrease of 12 per cent in steam consumption.

In helping to create these improved freight locomotives the value of the Altoona test plant cannot be over-emphasized. For here it was possible to produce data which gave the tests the preciseness and validity of a medical laboratory's compilations.

Following the tests of No. 790, the Pennsy built 122 engines of class Ils at Juniata. During the years 1922-1923, The Baldwin Locomotive Works

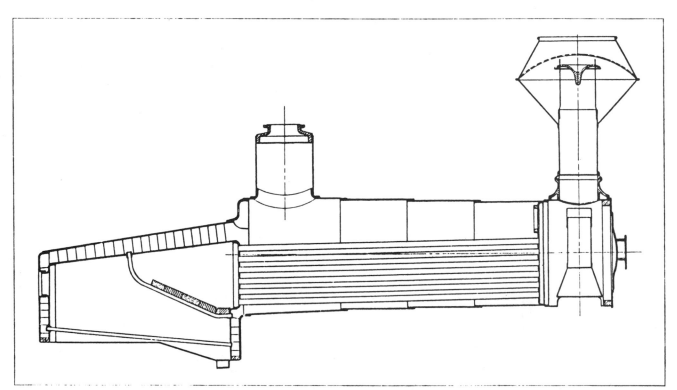

Altoona type boiler, as used on Class H1 (Old Class I). This drawing shows the short smoke box and diamond stack as used in 1875 and for several years thereafter. Brick arch in firebox was a later addition. It is shown on an official drawing of the Class H1 boiler dated August 3, 1909, and is here included as a matter of interest.

One of the Altoona built Consolidations, class H1, originally class I. Engine No. 128 ran on the Pennsy's Northern Central Railway. A novel feature of this class was the Altoona type boiler which was quite unlike those of other Pennsy engines. The boiler was of the straight-top form with its steam dome in front of the firebox, which latter had its roof sheet 9½ inches below the top of the boiler barrel. Crown and roof sheets both sloped toward the rear at a sharp angle with a narrowing space between them almost entirely filled with water. In such an arrangement there was little steam liberating surface above the firebox. Both crown and roof sheets were flat, and were stayed throughout by screw stays. When these locomotives went into service in 1875, Pennsy officials, naturally enough, wanted to find out their ability to do the job for which they were designed, and very important, how economically they could do it when compared to other engines in freight service. A lengthy fuel test was made between Altoona and Harrisburg, then 135 miles apart. A former Baldwin man recalled that he was assigned to keep notes on the weight of coal consumed, train weight, running time, record delays, steam pressure at intervals of five minutes, and the weight of ashes at the end of the run. None of the later day apparatus for a more refined method of testing was then available, but it was possible nonetheless, to get a good appraisal of their economy in service. They did exceptionally well, and for their day represented a decided advance over previous locomotives used in this same service.

Collection—Fred Westing

built 475 class Ils units with a more sophisticated approach. These locomotives were based on the original group, but were equipped with such items as feedwater heaters, power reverse gears and mechanical stokers of the Duplex type. Round-cased headlights replaced the square-cased design, and two large air drums were mounted over the pilot beam in place of the two originally located under the right hand running board. Crossheads and guides were also changed, being a development of Axel Vogt's guides used on the D14a

class engines of 1894. The smoke lifter used on the early K4s and L1s engines was retained. Another detail on the Juniata engines was their use of "A" type superheaters with top headers, while the Baldwin engines used "E" type superheaters with right and left headers in the smokebox.

During the years between 1912 and 1919, several Mallets of various types came on the Pennsy. They were, however, sparsely represented, for the Pennsy felt no pressing need or desire to acquire such gargantuan machines.

Built for moderately heavy fast freight service class F1a did good work. Later they were assigned to "work extras" for track maintenance gangs, and wreck trains.

Class F3 Mogul built by Baldwin in 1901. These engines used the round-top or radial-stay firebox.

A memorable run was made by this Pennsy Consolidation type locomotive of class R (later class H3c) No. 263 built at Fort Wayne Shops in 1892 for the Pittsburgh, Fort Wayne & Chicago Railway. In that same year No. 263 hauled a forty car freight train loaded with 2,640,000 pounds of grain between Chicago and Philadelphia, a distance of 824 miles. Engine and cars were equipped with Westinghouse brakes, and the locomotive was not once uncoupled from the train during the run. Helper engines were used at certain points as follows; Pittsburgh to Derry, 46 miles, Conemaugh to Gallitzin over the mountains, 25 miles, Columbia to 42nd street, Philadelphia, and over the Arsenal bridge. Leaving Chicago at 10 a.m. on April 30, 1892, the train arrived at the Girard Point grain elevator on May 4th at 4:22 p.m. having covered the 824 miles in four days, 6½ hours. Weight of the train including engine and tender plus an 18,000 pound caboose, was 4,030,500 pounds. Originally old class R when first built it probably received an H3a classification, though later re-classified as an H3c, and I believe, renumbered 7263. Note the "bootleg" stack and the clerestory roof on top of the cab. This latter was a feature of this subclass. The stack was just 1½ inches short of five feet above the smokebox top. An engine of class H3a No. 292, was the first locomotive built in the then new Juniata Shops in July 1891.

Backhead of a class R, or newer class H3 designation. Note absence of backboards, but class H3a on Lines West had them. As usual on most Pennsy steam power, the backhead had a clean uncluttered appearance. Engine was No. 1187, built at Altoona Shops, 1888, shop number 1235.

View from fireman's side of engine No. 1187.

This H3 class engine No. 1195, built at Altoona Shops in 1888, was busy hauling freight trains in the 1890's. The bootleg stack had been replaced from its old class R days, and a trap-door ventilator was used on the cab roof top.

A class H2, No. 7904, which was featured on the Lines West. Built at the Allegheny Shops in May 1890, it was originally numbered PFW&CRR No. 253.

Class H3c engine No. 7906, built at Fort Wayne Shops, October 1892. When built this locomotive's tender bore the initials PFW&C RW.

An H6b class Consolidation No. 2906, built by Baldwin in 1905, construction number 26,863. These engines represented the first prolific application of Walschaerts gear and piston valve cylinders on the Pennsy. Great prosperity was on the land when these locomotives came out, and Baldwin was swamped with locomotive orders. Their shops were working 24 hours around the clock, and they needed to, for between October 10, and November 22, 1905, Baldwin built 160 Pennsy class H6b engines. During the years 1905 to 1907, Baldwin turned out a total of 423 such locomotives. Years later many of the H6b engines had superheaters applied to them and became class H6sb, the letter "s" indicating this action.

An H6b and an H6a of the Philadelphia Division, labor up the big fill between Narberth and Wynnewood, Pa., in 1908, with a long trailing line of empty hopper cars bound for the coal mines. The leading engine, class H6b, No. 3219, was built by Baldwin in December 1907, construction number 32,376. Around 1909-1910, its number was changed to 728, and in 1911 it was assigned to the New Jersey Division. Engine No. 728 was equipped with a Schmidt superheater in 1917, and scrapped in 1939. When this engine was built it was probably coupled to that large 70-F-70 class tender, because by 1907 these tenders were being used by the large H8 class locomotives which made their appearance in 1907. The train is passing bracket-post automatic signal A-18.

Engine No. 2, of the New York, Philadelphia & Norfolk Railroad, hauling a freight train over the road that later became the Delmarva Division of the Pennsy. Engine No. 2, was built by Baldwin in April 1895, construction number 14,270, and was of the 4-6-0 type with 18″ × 24″ cylinders, and 62″ drivers. It was typical of many ten-wheelers of that period particularly the wagon-top boiler with its narrow firebox. Note the Pennsy's Union Line box car with its prominent red star trademark in the white circle.

Engine No. 340, class G4 ten-wheeler, or 4-6-0 type assigned to the Pittsburgh Cincinnati Chicago & St. Louis Railroad. These engines were in their day noted for their clean cut lines. On the Pittsburgh Division they showed exceptional ability in combating the grades that led to the Horseshoe Curve, from the east and the west.

135

Engine 5724 class G5s, hauling westbound excursion train through Linden N. J., May 1, 1931. Train had 21 cars in consist.

Baldwin built K4s No. 5406 heads the westbound ''Golden Arrow'' on part of its run to Chicago.

A Pennsy Lines West class H8a engine built at Juniata December 1907. This engine was originally numbered 7509 before becoming No. 7501 as shown. While appearing quite similar, the H8 and its sub-classes did have some external differences that set them apart from classes H9s and H10s. For example, class H9s had a superheater and outside steam pipes with vacuum relief valves on top of each steam chest which were part of the outside steam pipes. Instead of a single stage 9½ inch air compressor on each side one 8½ inch cross-compound air compressor on the left side was used. The two safety valves, one on each side of the steam dome was placed on top of the firebox roof sheet. On the H8a the Vogt vacuum relief valve was still in use. And for reversing the engine the old lever and quadrant was used. Spoked wheels were still used on this engine's pony truck, and coupled to the engine was a 70-F-70 tender which was used with many of these engines east and west of Pittsburgh.

A triple header made up of one H6a and two H8 class locomotives blast their way eastward near Radnor, Pa., in 1911, with a heavy coal train. The leading engine No. 2546, was built by Baldwin in March 1905 at the old Spring Garden Street Works in Philadelphia.

Engine No. 313 class H9s built by Baldwin at Eddystone August 1913, construction number 40,346. Safety valves are on top of firebox roof sheet, but whistle was still connected to steam dome. Reason, safety valves when "popping off" had tendency to draw water into throttle valve when open. Pennsy did not, however, like putting more holes in boiler either, but of two evils roof sheet pop valves seemed the lesser. Low-sided tender class 70-F-70a is coupled to engine, and new design vacuum relief or snifter valve was placed on top of valve chests forming part of the outside steam pipes. Instead of lever and quadrant reverse a screw was used with reach rod above running board. A metal pilot beam with indented push-pole pockets, one per side formed part of the wooden pilot.

With Edward R. Carlson at the throttle, a big Juniata Shops H8b class Consolidation built in 1911, and numbered 1093 passes North Elizabeth, N.J., on July 27, 1913. The train had just left Waverly Yard, a short distance east, and is on its westbound run. The grade from Waverly Yard to North Elizabeth is quite noticeable, and the train is still climbing to raise it over the Central Railroad of New Jersey four track crossing at the eastern end of Elizabeth Station. Note the bridge "ticklers" to warn trainman who might be on top of the cars at the overhead bridge. To permit freight trains to come out on the main line without blocking eastbound passenger trains on track No. 1, an ascending grade on this track brought trains to a "jumpover" bridge so that east and westbound freight trains could pass in and out of Waverly Yard without interference. Engineer Carlson "went running" regularly in October 1912 after years of firing. He often fired for Martin Lee on the Manhattan Transfer-Washington runs and Lee considered him a first-rate fireman.

A right side view of a Lines West class H10s Consolidation No. 8089 built by Baldwin in December 1913, construction number 40,997. You can see that a straight line running board replaced the two-level arrangement used on the H9s on the road east of Pittsburgh. The main reservoir of smaller diameter was required to clear chassis details. The H9s with its running boards raised at a higher level toward the front of the locomotive were able to use a shorter reservoir of larger diameter. This engine was superheated and used the screw reverse gear operated by a dished handwheel in the cab. Safety valves, as was quite customary, were encased in an auxiliary dome on top of the firebox roof sheet.

Collection—Fred Westing

A left side view of H10s class engine No. 9710 built by Baldwin. The arrangement on this side shows the two 9½ inch single stage air compressors which was a feature of Lines West practice for many years. The built up inverted metal section raised above the low-sided tender collar was typical of Lines West, and this specific tender was known as class 7B, Fort Wayne route. Later its classification was changed to 80-F-81. This engine was stoker fired and the steam cylinder for operating the stoker can be seen under the cab. Inventor of this stoker was David F. Crawford, General Superintendent of Motive Power, Lines West. Mr. Crawford later became General Manager of the Pennsy's Lines West, and then went with the Locomotive Stoker Company as a Vice President.

A near flat-side view of the first L1s class locomotive No. 1752, built in April 1914, at Juniata Shops. Due to a lower boiler centerline the stack in order to utilize the full fifteen feet of clearance was somewhat taller than that of the K4s class engine built one month later. Otherwise, the boilers of both classes were identical. The first L1s had its sandbox placed in back of the bell and used a low-sided tender. On following Mikados the sandbox was placed behind the stack quite near to it and ahead of the bell. A tender with a higher collar and greater coal and water capacity was coupled to these engines for some years after. The smoke-lifter pipe of one inch diameter, which fed steam to an opening in the stack's rim is plainly visible. The vacuum relief valve was placed alongside each valve chest as on the E6s engines, and for some time after on the L1s and K4s engines.

A **more acute angle view** of No. 1752 showing the rim-stack smoke-lifter in action. The old style square case headlight used on much Pennsy power both freight and passenger until well into the 1920's is part of this big "Mike's" equipment. Kerosene oil was used to provide the light until around 1917, when electric steam-turbine generators powered a 200 watt bulb in the headlight.

A **Baldwin L1s** No. 1372 built in July 1918, construction number 49,424. This engine represented a newer arrangement of some details with vacuum relief valves on top of the steam chests, and the use of two smokebox braces with one step each changed it from the original form. Many such items, such as the casing outside the cab's right side, and arrangement of the running boards were duplicated on the K4s Pacifics, plus retention of the wooden pilot. The casing housed part of the screw reverse gear mechanism, thereby permitting a smaller cab.

Engine No. 906 class L1s, built by Baldwin in January 1916, construction number 42,750, as it emerged from the Eddystone erecting shop. After 1912 the larger sized locomotives were built at the Eddystone, Pa. Plant rather than at 500 North Broad Street, Philadelphia. This engine was still using a wooden pilot, tail rods, and vacuum relief, or drifting valves, at sides of steam chests. Another item used on the first L1s, No. 1752, was carried over on No. 906 which was the first of many "Mikes" built for the Pennsy, and that was the steam pipe arrangement for feeding the 8½ inch cross compound air compressor. Note that steam was fed directly from a steam turret inside the cab (not visible in picture) and not from the steam dome as was done on many later engines of this class. The only K4s Pacific that fed steam to the compressor from a turret inside the cab was, I believe, the first K4s No. 1737. I have seen K4s engines built in 1917 and 1918 when new, and recall that their compressors obtained steam from the steam dome. In place of a low-sided tender one with a higher collar with more fuel and water capacity was used and known as class 90-F-66. These were the standard tenders for the L1s engines, but many years later the original collar was added to, and flared inwardly.

Engine 4699, built in October 1923, by Baldwin at Eddystone, construction number 57317. Between 1922-1923, Baldwin built 475 of these class I1s Decapods for the Pennsy. The first of this vast number was No. 4300 built November 1922, construction number 55,725. Like the engine illustrated it embodied many items that were absent on the first Pennsy built I1s of 1916, No. 790. All the 475 units that emerged from Eddystone's huge erecting shop, were equipped with Worthington feedwater heaters, Duplex stokers, power reverse gears, and one 8½ inch cross-compound air pump. New arrangement of the main reservoirs or drums, with two supported in front of the smokebox. The smoke lifter pipe, however, was still being used. Chassis details also differed in some respects from the 1916 engines; a new crosshead with duplex guides replaced the two-bar guides with alligator crossheads. A new design of link hanger for the Walschaerts gear was in evidence, and the non-lifting injectors on the left side as used on the K4s engines and class HC1s took some piping off the backhead where room was needed for the two large conveyor tubes of the mechanical stoker. New tenders class 90-F-82, were originally coupled to these Baldwin built I1s locomotives. The method whereby the engine cut-off was 50 per cent in full gear was retained.

Collection—Fred Westing

An experimental I1s Decapod, No. 4525 with Baldwin two-flow cylinders built in August 1923, construction number 56,869. Like all Baldwin I1s engines it was equipped with the "E" type superheater instead of the "A" type applied to the Altoona built jobs. From the dome's left side a pipe fed saturated steam to the air compressor. This piping arrangement was used on the K4s class and later the pipe was placed at the rear of the dome, but in the twilight years of the K4 the Pennsy reverted to running the pipe to the compressor from a connection to the left side of the steam dome.

Empty hopper cars returning to the coal mines round the Horseshoe Curve with a Baldwin built I1s at the head end. On this section the going was rough and the engineer had to run on a long cut-off. That is where the 50 per cent cut-off in full gear paid off and produced money saving economies.

Fred Westing

Front end of the first Baldwin built I1s. Two main air drums are supported on two bracket castings. Push pole pockets, one per side, are embedded in the pilot beam casting similar to those used on the old and newer Consolidations of the Pennsy.

Back end and cab interior of engine 4300. The barrel type coal conveyors of the Duplex stoker take up quite some room. Injector check is shown at left side of backhead. In those days Pennsy still clung to the sight-feed lubricator on fireman's side. Throttle lever is readily discernible. Keeping the boiler supplied with water was primarily the job of the feedwater heater, while the fireman took care of the non-lifting injector on his side of the engine. There was no outside steam pipe for an injector on the right-hand side of these Baldwin I1s locomotives.

A couple of Decapod pushers approach the east end of Gallitzin tunnel as they help lift a heavy freight train about 1,000 feet from Altoona to Gallitzin in less than twelve miles. The two tunnels are at the crest of the mountain. Through the westbound tunnel are two tracks, and one through the eastbound bore. Trains approaching the tunnels from either direction have to climb a western or eastern slope, but the westbound grade is more severe. A ventilating system powered by large fans did its best to clear the tunnels of noxious fumes.

Westbound empties approaching Gallitzin tunnel on the Pittsburgh Division. That huge tender carried plenty of water and coal to meet the demands of the Baldwin I1s. A cabin at the rear of the tender housed the head-end brakeman, and was provided with steam heat when needed. This tender with two eight-wheel trucks was known as class 210-F-84, which meant that it had a water capacity of 21,000 gallons, while the letter "F" indicated that it was used in freight service, and measured 84¼ inches from the rail top to the deck plate. Originally applied to the class J1 2-10-4 type locomotives, they had a coal capacity of around 30 tons.

Engine 4493, a Baldwin I1s built in May 1923, construction number 56,554, makes a momentary halt as her engine crew obligingly pose for their picture. This photo gives a good view of much of the piping and the valve gear's novel link supporting casting.

A United States Railroad Administration engine No. 7139, their class 2-10-2B, Pennsy class N2s. This was one of the USRA engines built by Baldwon at Eddystone in July 1919, construction number 52,093, for the Pennsylvania Railroad, Lines West. By this time coaches and tenders were lettered Pennsylvania Lines to indicate equipment used on the road west of Pittsburgh. This locomotive of the 2-10-2 or Santa Fe type where it originated, was decidedly not Pennsy in appearance. Baker valve gear replaced Walschaerts, two sandboxes were used instead of one, and the steam turbine-electric generator was placed on top of a radial-stay, or round-top firebox, in place of the usual Pennsy location behind the stack. In steam's twilight years on the Pennsy the generator was supported on a bracket placed on the smokebox front. Later the N2s engines were fitted with Belpaires fireboxes, and one sandbox replaced two. As thus modified they became the Pennsy's class N2sa.

In 1919 the Pennsy built at their Juniata Shops an enormous single-expansion articulated, or simple Mallet locomotive of the 2-8-8-0 type known as class HC1s, and bearing road number 3700. It was to be used only for pusher service on the Pittsburgh Division, and subsequently fulfilled that mission. The boiler was exceptionally large, and featured a Belpaire firebox and combustion chamber of unusual design and construction. The first boiler course was conical on top with a minimum outside diameter of 96 inches, while the second course was straight and measured 110 inches for the outside diameter. The long stretch of the shoulders, or hips, of the firebox roof sheet, were due to the lengthy barrel combustion chamber of 11 feet 7¾ inches. The firebox itself was 14 feet in length. In order to provide for expansion of this long combustion chamber the throat sheet connection with the firebox was made with a fold or corrugation. Years later, this same form and construction procedure of firebox and combustion chamber was applied to the M1 class Mountain type locomotives successfully. Four separate stacks were embodied in one single casting which, while giving it an oversize look conformed to more conventional practice. The reason for using four stacks was to obtain a satisfactory ratio of stack diameter to length. Engine 3700 was fired by a Duplex mechanical stoker, and had a Franklin powered grate shaker. A Schmidt "E" type superheater was used, and two non-lifting injectors with a steam pipe outside the cab on each side which fed steam from an outside steam turret to the injector's starting valve. This same arrangement appeared on fifty K4s class locomotives in 1920 numbered 3726 to 3775. The bridge pipe that carried saturated steam from the steam dome to the outside turret which was enclosed in a metal casing was a detail later appropriated by class M1. Reversal of the locomotive was accomplished by a hydro-pneumatic reverse gear. To obtain economical results similar to that of class I1s when operating at slow speed in full gear the same method of cutting off the steam at half stroke, or 50 per cent was adopted. At the yearly convention of the American Railway Master Mechanics' Association held at Atlantic City in 1919, this locomotive with its awesome size held the attention and interest of the many who viewed it.

Another view of the Prosperity Special getting ready to leave on its long trek to the west coast. Engine No. 121, class L1s built at Juniata in 1917, is at the head end. The metal shielding over the lower metal pilot slats was used on many K4s class Pacifics as well as the L1s class. Note engine is still using tailrods at the forward end of the cylinders, but the vacuum relief valves have been relocated on top of the valve chests and form part of the outside steam pipes.

Collection—Fred Westing

The author points to the vacuum relief valve on M1a class engine No. 6759.

In 1921 the Southern Pacific Company ordered 50 locomotives of the 2-10-2 type. These engines were completed in 1922, and Samuel Vauclain thought this a fine opportunity to provide a demonstration of American industry. A group of twenty of these giant locomotives were, therefore, herded together to form a train that was known as the Prosperity Special. Leaving the Baldwin Eddystone Plant on May 26, 1922, the train moved over the Pennsylvania Railroad to East St. Louis, and was there delivered to the St. Louis-Southwestern RR., or "Cotton Belt Route" which took the train to Corsicana, Texas. From that point the train traveled over the Southern Pacific to Los Angeles, Cal., where it arrived on July 4th, 1922, after covering a distance of 3,743 miles. Much publicity was given to this unique gesture of American prosperity, and many thousands of people viewed the train as it passed on its way. The picture shows the train moving south headed by two L1s class engines as it passes under the signal bridge at the northern end of the Baldwin, Pa. station at Baldwin's Eddystone Works.

A "saddle tanker" class A29, formerly class Pg, built at the Fort Wayne Shops of the PFW&C in November 1879. It was later renumbered 7109, and became known as a tank engine of the A29 class. This photo was taken in 1910, and in 1912 the engine was scrapped. This locomotive was a loner, and represented the only one of its class.

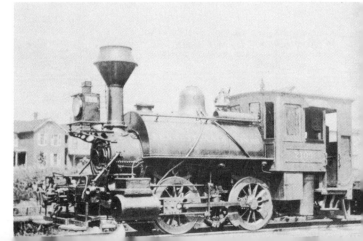

Scene on Delaware Avenue Philadelphia, near South Street. A Pennsy 0-4-0 type switcher in foreground; originally class "U" later class A3. These engines had slope-back tenders with a large headlight at rear of tank.

A saddle-tank engine of the 0-4-0 type, class Q2, later class A2, built around 1885, and very active in the 1890's.

150

Former class M, No. 7130 of the 0-6-0 type used for switching on the P.F.W.&C. Ry. Built at Altoona in June 1885, as No. 130, it was later known as class B3, when this part of the road became known as Pennsylvania Lines West.

Built for the P.F.W.&C. Ry. at its Fort Wayne Shops, in December 1883, as a class H1 and numbered 7067, as a locomotive of the Consolidation type. Later converted into class C29 by removal of the pony truck. Engine operated on Pennsylvania Lines as No. 7067, and ended its days as No. 10067.

Engine 5235 of the Maryland Division, class B4a. The original 0-6-0 type class M design was revised in 1891, and equipped with a Belpaire firebox, thereby creating class B4. In 1893, with an increase in firebox size, the design became class B4a, which appears to have operated only on lines east of Pittsburgh.

Class B8, built at Juniata in 1904. Picture taken in West Philadelphia. A slope-back tank, and clerestory cab ventilator were features of this class. Note location of bell just ahead of cab which was characteristic of switch engines built after 1900.

Engine No. 1042, class B8, built by Baldwin in January 1904, construction number 23,490. This locomotive was assigned to the New York Division, and was in active service for some time after 1920.

Class A5s, built at Altoona as were all engines of this class. First made their appearance in 1916, and were all superheater equipped when built. With their comparatively short wheelbase these engines proved most suitable in the Philadelphia area where they encountered many sharp curves and limited clearances among the numerous industrial sidings encountered in the day's work.

Chapter 9

Martin H. Lee
New York Division Engineman

In this Chapter are described the activities that befell a locomotive engineer on the Pennsy many years ago. Some of the locomotives he drove and for which he had special affection are illustrated. Also shown are photos taken by his friend Charles B. Chaney, when riding the cab of Lee's engines.

Captions explain the pictures for, despite the Chinese proverb that "A picture is worth a thousand words" it is only when supplemented by the written or verbal word that a deeper understanding is obtained.

Martin Lee was born at Turtle Creek, Pa., January 14, 1860. His father was a railroader, and soon young Martin was working as a water boy with a track gang. From there he went to wiping engines at Mantua roundhouse, and after a good spell he applied for a job as fireman on the New York Division, December 8, 1879. On that same day he went firing and recalled that it was a cold and rainy Monday.

From then until December 16, 1882, he fired freight and passenger trains, and on December 17, 1882, took his first freight train from Mantua in West Philadelphia, to Harsimus Cove, Jersey City, with New York, West Shore, & Buffalo Railway Company engine No. 56. The train was made up of stock cars, and as usual ran as an extra. It left Mantua at 2 p.m., and arrived at Harsimus Cove, on the Hudson River just north of the Pennsy passenger terminal, at 6:50 p.m. Return run was with the same engine from the Meadows at 6:40 a.m., next day, and arrived at Mantua 10:30 a.m. This train was made up of one dead engine and 26 empties.

At last in the coveted place on the right-hand side of the cab with his hand on the throttle, on May 1, 1887, on an old class P, later D11a class, Lee went into passenger service on a Broad Street-Trenton, run. He made two round trips that day which was a sort of a "swing shift" job with layovers, that kept him working from 9:07 a.m., until 7:34 p.m. But on March 29, 1888, he drew a through passenger run from Broad Street Station, to Jersey City with the second section of train 42, the Southern and New York Express. The train left Broad Street at 9:20 p.m., and arrived at Jersey City 11:28 p.m. The engine he drove was No. 1067, old class K, later reclassified as a D6 in the 1890's.

Lee, however, was still "bucking the extra board" and frequently went back on freight runs. It was not until November 30, 1891, that he went into regular passenger service, and he did it running a top-name train, No. 8, then the Pennsy's "Day Express." On that November day, with engine No. 184, a K class engine with 78-inch drivers, he pulled out of Broad Street at 7:13 p.m., with the second section (second No. 8) of this speedy daylight train that ran daily between Pittsburgh and New York. Train 8 arrived at Jersey City, 9:27 p.m. His fireman was E. A. Jacobson, and the conductor, George W. Brown.

From then on until August 16, 1908, Lee ran various passenger trains between Philadelphia and Jersey city, and return which constituted the normal day's work. He usually worked one Sunday per month.

In 1879, Martin Lee began his engine service career as a fireman on a locomotive of this type. Contrast this class G1, 4-6-0 type Altoona product with the big E6s class engines he drove 35 years later. A push-pole is on the side of the tender under the tank, and the pilot has the typical metal slats of a "chicken coop" design long used on Pennsy power.

One exception to this routine was when for about half the month of June in 1902, he ran the "Pennsylvania Special" which he had the honor to operate on its first westbound and eastbound trips over the New York Division. Here is how it came about. On March 23, 1902, with 15 minutes notice, Lee was asked to take a two-car "Special" carrying Pennsy President, Alexander Johnston Cassatt, over the New York Division, from Broad Street to Jersey City. He was given engine No. 804, class D16a, which was according to Lee, not in the best condition. But despite losing five minutes due to signal slowdowns, and observing the speed restriction through the streets of Newark, N.J., where the Pennsy ran at street level, he made the run in 79 minutes, start to stop. Mr. Cassatt was so impressed that when the speedy 20-hour Pennsylvania Special was first put into service on June 15, 1902, he requested that Lee initiate this train service which he did until relinquishing it to men with greater seniority.

On February 26, 1903, Lee drove another "Special" over the Division. This time Samuel Spencer, President of the Southern Railway was the distinguished passenger in his Southern Railway private car No. 212. For the Pennsy train crew a "set-up" or "rider" car was provided making a light load for the single-domed E2 No. 1985. Lee covered the 59 miles from Philadelphia to New Brunswick in 42 minutes. It can be seen that the E2 was eating up those miles, so fast in fact that the Division Superintendent had the train stopped as for some time Lee had been averaging 85 mph. He was told to

slow down, and that an 86 minute run over the line would be preferred. Nonetheless, Lee with a speed reduction handicap made the run in 79 minutes.

Three years later, on November 29, 1906, President Spencer was killed while riding in his private car on the Southern Railway, near Lawyers, Va., 11 miles south of Lynchburg. His train, No. 33, was struck from the rear by train 37, the southbound New York & New Orleans Limited. His car being the last, was greatly damaged, and several other passengers within it were also killed.

Lee also inaugurated the first westbound run of train No. 23, later called the Manhattan Limited, though when first operated it was called the Chicago Limited. From the start, however, the eastbound section, train 22, was known as the Manhattan Limited. For over one year Lee handled train 23, on his homebound run, but he went east on train No. 44, the Washington, Philadelphia and New York Express. On this first trip which took place Sunday, May 24, 1903, Lee had engine 1435, class E2. On train 23 he had D16a class engine No. 280 quite frequently and it did a fine job despite this all-Pullman train. Train 23 ran via Broad Street Station, but by 1907, it ran through the New York-Pittsburgh subway and bypassed old Broad Street. A splendid record for punctuality was made by Lee with train 23, and on this run he also occasionally had engine 88, the first of the D16a class engines.

After going into the Manhattan Transfer-Washington service at the end of November 1910, Lee had nothing but light Atlantics on trains 59 and

56. Sometimes he had other trains but finally the Congressional Limited and combined FFV and New York and New Orleans Limited were his steady runs until the end of his career. He used to refer to the C&O's "FFV" as the "Canary Line" due to the distinctive orange and yellow blend coloring of the cars. It was a beautiful train and I had the pleasure of seeing it several times on the Pennsy.

At last on March 19, 1914, Lee drove his first Pacific. It was engine No. 5183, class K2sa built in 1912 at Juniata, and assigned to the Maryland Division. With this engine he headed train 56 to Manhattan Transfer, and then headed for the Meadows enginehouse from which point most of the runs began and ended since leaving Waldo Avenue enginehouse, in Jersey City. His fireman on that K2 run was Nelson P. Robelard.

From then on with few exceptions, he had a steady supply of K2 locomotives; some were superheated and some were not. On June 1st, 1914, Lee and fireman Joe Garrett got a new 1914 built E6s, No. 737, for trains 59 and 56. This was an assigned engine with another new E6s No. 779, as a relief engine. At rare intervals they got a K2 but until the end of his career the engine used by him on these trains were mostly of the E6s class.

In April 1915 Lee had two unusual experiences. On the 10th of that month, train 56 arrived at Manhattan Transfer 10 hours late. This was due to a bad wreck that occurred on the C&O and the "FFV" from Cincinnati to New York, had to detour about 200 miles at reduced speed. The train arrived 10 hours late at Washington, and Lee's E6s engine 779 had gone north with another train. He had, however, engine 1281, also an E6s, and while he did not lose time, could not make up any. He arrived home in Philadelphia about 4:30 a.m. Then on the 16th of the same month, due to a Pennsy wreck at Odenton, Md., he ran train 56 over the B&O from Washington to Baltimore with engine 737, which was probably the only E6s that had this distinction. Norman H. MacDonald was his fireman in both instances.

His last trip was made on May 13th, 1915, when he brought train 56 into the "Transfer" for the last time with engine 779. Shortly after his arrival home he became very ill and required immediate medical attention. On July 11, 1915, he passed away fulfilling a prophecy he had made to a close friend; "Engine 779 was the last I will ever turn a wheel on; I've crossed the pike for the last time." An exceptionally sad sequel was the death of his eldest daughter Mary, which followed that of her father just two hours later.

Many were the mourners at the double funeral for father and daughter for both had many friends. Lee's friends were not only those numbered among his fellow workers, but those who rode the Congressional Limited, and recalled the ever present kindly smile and the smooth-shaven face topped with silver locks as they passed the panting engine at Washington's Union Station. Neither the New York Division, or the Pennsylvania Railroad ever replaced Martin Lee.

Engine No. 1395 class D16a, at Atlantic City, N.J. This was one of three locomotives that differed from others of its class by having 7-inch valve travel, and longer links. They proved to be speedy runners, and this, no doubt, influenced the use of 1395 on the Pennsylvania Special on the first westbound run and subsequent "break-in" runs in 1902.

Of all the D16a class engines that Lee drove, No. 903 was his favorite. ''She's great'' he would say with genuine affection. This scene shows 903 hauling train No. 98, then a Philadelphia-New York express. First two cars are Pullmans with two coaches and one combination car on fhe rear. Picture was taken near Rahway, N.J., in 1896. Lee once made 102 mph with this locomotive speeding between Metuchen and Rahway. His fireman on that run, and in this picture was Belleville Graham.

In 1895 Lee made many a round trip between Philadelphia and Jersey City, with engine No. 1510. This locomotive was built in 1892, by the Baldwin Locomotive Works, in Philadelphia. It was a 4-cylinder Vauclain compound. Lee's fireman on most of these runs was Flavel Smith, who later became one of the best enginemen on the New York Division.

The prestige of the Pennsy was resting on engine 1395, and her engine crew that day of June 15, 1902. For across the Hudson River in New York City, on this very afternoon, the New York Central & Hudson River Railroad, from Grand Central Terminal, were inaugurating their competitive "Twentieth Century Limited" on the same 20-hour schedule between the two cities of New York and Chicago. The Central were using a larger engine of the Atlantic type, but engineer Lee, at the extreme left had no qualms nor did fireman Bob Timby, second from the left. Cars in following order from the engine were, Pullman sleeping cars, Tyrone and Chile, Pennsy Dining Car, and Combination Car, named Utopia. In this latter car one could be attended by a barber and obtain a bath. In the baggage compartment were located the facilities for providing electricity to light the complete train and replenish the storage batteries. At Powelton Avenue, West Philadelphia, 1395 was uncoupled and another D16a, No. 96, coupled to the Combination Car Utopia, at the other end of the train. Thus the train consist was reversed, and the first car out of Jersey City, was the last car into Chicago. From Philadelphia to Harrisburg, No. 96, had engineer H. M. Hinkle, and fireman W. H. McKeen, for the engine crew. The train itself brought forth such colorful expressions as the "Red Ripper" the "Streak of Red" and the "Red Demon". This was due to the train's external appearance, resplendent in its Pennsy standard Tuscan red coloring. All this made for eye-catching front page publicity, which was ably handled by Col. F. N. Barksdale, Pennsy's Advertising Agent, who rode the train on its first westbound run.

Train 29, the Pennsylvania Special, shortly after leaving the big train shed in Jersey City. From Jersey City to Newark, the Pennsy main line comprised two separate double-tracked lines; one for freight and one for passenger service. Train 29 is on the westbound track speeding to Newark. To the left of the picture are two tracks, east and westbound for freight traffic. These freight trains by-passed the passenger line to Newark, and made connection with the four-track main line at Waverly, N.J. This picture was taken on the first run of the Pennsylvania Special westbound, on June 15, 1902, as the train passed Caledonia Park in Jersey City.

NOT
CARD

to Care
nd Steam-
wded

opright, 1902.
pany.
Charles W.
mong the ar-
terday. Mr.
ondon for the
bout the end
ater he will
rough France.
ans are com-
ge numbers,"
at the Carl
to get choice
Celtic sailed
re than two-
One usually
ion crowd at
many New
ey care much

didn't think
t field for
ow.
Englishmen
nst American
s a rule, look
es over here.
nglicised, it is
rorable recep-

SHAFT

ed and Fell

the bakery,
treets, yester-
nith, aged 45
falling down

e bakery and
t the elevator
nd fell head-
e block of ice
was taken to
e patrol from
n streets sta-
arrived there
home at 3047

Asleep

yesterday at
ged 26 years,
iked through
ing-room door
His face and
vhile his neck
He was taken
al, where the
vill require an
es.

ng vs. Renting

r to buy a home, paying for it a little at a time,
rent year after year and have nothing to show for it?

NEW EIGHTEEN-HOUR TRAIN
ON RECORD-BREAKING RUN

Pennsylvania Railroad's Long-Distance Flyer Left Germantown Junction Yesterday Afternoon and Is Expected to Reach Chicago This Morning

EIGHTEEN HOUR FLYER AT GERMANTOWN JUNCTION

Germantown Junction Station was crowded with people yesterday afternoon to witness the arrival of the Pennsylvania Railroad's initial flyer running from New York to Chicago in twenty hours. The train, composed of an engine and four cars, arrived on schedule time, 3.44, and after taking on a coterie of Philadelphia newspaper men ran into Powelton avenue yard, where it changed crew and engines, and started on its long run west.

All along the route between Philadelphia and Harrisburg the station platforms were lined with people who cheered the fast moving train. Frequently the engineer slowed down, finding he was making better time than the schedule called for. The ease with which the speed was maintained leaves little doubt that this train, officially known as No. 29, will readily reduce by four hours the time between Chicago and the East. Had the maximum speed been sustained the flyer would have reached Harrisburg ahead of time, but by slowing down Engineer Hinkle took his train into the State capital at 5.50, as per schedule. It is expected to reach Chicago at 8.55 o'clock this morning by central time, which is two hours later than Philadelphia time.

CENTRAL'S NEW FLYER

Special to The Inquirer.

NEW YORK, June 15.—The New York Central's new flyer, the "Twentieth Century Limited," left New York on its maiden trip at 2.45 this afternoon. Every seat was taken when the limited pulled out of the Grand Central Station, its wheels exploding torpedoes which a trainman had placed on the track for luck. John W. Gates, of Chicago, went out on the train.

SYRACUSE, N. Y., June 15.—The New York Central's new flyer, which left New York on its maiden trip this afternoon, at a late hour to-night gave every indication of keeping to its schedule time and landing its passengers at Chicago twenty hours after they left New York. The run to Albany was scheduled to take one hour and fifty minutes, and there the train was five minutes ahead of time. Syracuse was reached exactly on schedule.

REV. YERKES QUITS   HANSON HINTS AT

Lee and his fireman John P. Carlin, on the Meadows ready track with engine No. 1028, class E3sd. This was another former E3d converted into an E3sd with the application of a superheater. No. 1028 only had one 9½ inch, single stage air compressor in the location where they were originally applied on all the light Atlantics built up to 1910 and possibly after. During this time the Pennsy was going to solid disc wheels for the forward truck. Such wheels had made their appearance on class E3d engines built in 1910. As the engines came in for lengthy repairs, and the spoked pair of wheels showed exceptional wear, they would be replaced with a pair of disc type wheels, hence the unmatched pair on the forward truck of No. 1028. Date of picture was June 15, 1913.

Waiting for the signal to back up and couple to the Congressional Limited. Engine 2768, class E2a, built 1905, is on the steam locomotive storage track at the west end of Manhattan Transfer near former "N" interlocking tower. The two single-stage 9½ compressors were arranged in tandem to insure increased braking power for heavier trains made up of all-steel cars.

A grand old favorite on the New York Division, engine No. 10. It carried the number of her predecessor "Long Legged Ten" the first of Pennsy's famous class K engines. This gave No. 10 something to live up to and she did it well. Engine 10 hauled the best, often on the Congressional Limited and Pennsylvania Special, before supplanted by that Atlantic of Atlantics, class E6s. Martin Lee had this engine regularly in 1908, on trains 120 and 121. Train 120 was an "Accommodation" train making 17 stops between Broad Street and Jersey City, yet was only allowed twenty minutes more than the speedy "clockers." Returning to Philadelphia, No. 10 hauled No. 121, a clocker that took just one hour and forty-five minutes including three intermediate station stops to run from Jersey City to Broad Street Station. Samuel Rea, then Third Vice President of the Pennsy, who was frequently in New York City overseeing the construction of the New York Station of the railroad, used to have his private car No. 120, on the rear of the train. Engine No. 10, built at Altoona in 1908, was an E3d, using saturated (non-superheated) steam. It was equipped with a superheater in 1912. This locomotive worked trains between Jersey City and New Brunswick, until the erection of the catenary system when electrification took over, and possibly on work trains after that. Train had just passed North Elizabeth Station and was a favorite picture of Chaney's. Lee was at the throttle and Daniel J. Fitzpatrick was the fireman. Date was July 12, 1913.

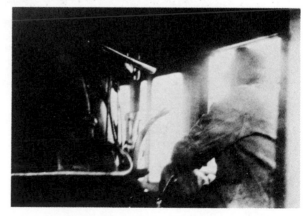

Martin Lee on the job in the cab of 2768. The curve of the right-hand injector lever is quite pronounced. The fireman's injector lever (not shown) was straight. In front of his hand is a vertical lever which is slanting forward. This was the straight-air brake valve or independent brake valve used to operate the brakes on engine and tender only. On newer Pennsy power this valve had its lever in a horizontal position similar to that of the automatic brake valve handle. In this picture the handle is in release position.

161

Coupled to the 7 car Congressional and ready to go. Engineer Lee faces Chaney's camera lens from the fireman's window, while fireman Charles P. Weigman leans from the gangway. An interested car inspector stands alongside the tender tank. Chaney rode this engine to Washington on Saturday afternoon August 23, 1913.

Engine 2768 is checked over at Washington, as Martin Lee gets it ready for the return trip home. Soon it will back up to the Washington Terminal Station to couple onto train No. 96, the Southern Railway Express. Date August 24, 1913.

In the cab of No. 2768. The two levers at top of picture are the throttle and whistle pull. The curved lever close at hand operated the engineer's injector, and ahead of it is the reverse lever almost in mid-gear position.

Lee's first K2. Engine 5183 of the Maryland Division, class K2sa (the "S" indicated superheater equipped) built at Juniata Shops, 1912. Lee had it on a northbound run with train 56, the date March 19, 1914. This locomotive like No. 2768, used two 9½ inch single stage air compressors in tandem instead of one 8½ inch cross-compound compressor which soon followed on all such big power.

Train 59, the Congressional Limited has just arrived at Manhattan Transfer after having passed under the Hudson River and speeded across the Jersey meadows over the high-line embankment which took the Pennsy over several railroads. This is a pet locomotive of the writer, for it was the first locomotive upon which he ever rode. It was No. 31 class DD1, mechanical parts built at Juniata Shops, electrical equipment supplied by Westinghouse. These locomotives were assembled and electrically equipped at the East Pittsburgh Works of the Westinghouse Electric & Manufacturing Company in 1910 and 1911.

With No. 737 coupled to the Congressional Limited and ready for the conductor's starting signal. Joe Garrett peers rather anxiously at Charlie Chaney as the signal is expected momentarily. Chaney rode the engine this day to Washington and returned the next day on train 56, same engine.

Next morning August 16th, 1914, Martin Lee checks the running gear and oils around as he did at the Meadows. The radius rod of the valve gear is in reverse as the engine will back down to the Washington Terminal Station to pick up train 56, the combined "FFV" of the C&O, and the Southern Railway's "New York and New Orleans Limited."

Engineman Lee oils No. 737 before heading for Manhattan Transfer. Take notice of the fine view of the crosshead and guide bars, also the step used at that time to help the engineer oil the upper parts of the valve gear.

Engine 737 has stopped at the water plug where fireman Joe Garrett is giving her tender tank a big drink. This is a fine side silhouette-like view of an E6s. The large sandbox which was used on the earlier engines was quite similar to that used on the big Consolidations then in service. There was one exception, however, most E6s engines had their sandbox filling lids placed right and left, while the Consolidations all had theirs front and back. In fact, I never saw an H8, H9s, or H10s and their subclasses, with right and left sandbox lids. A few E6s engines followed this "fore and aft" arrangement. Soon 737 will head for the Transfer.

A full view of engine and tender while Lee the careful engineer goes over his Iron Horse, with meticulous attention to details. Joe Garrett rests in the cab, for once they get rolling his duties will keep him active. But Joe told Chaney who rode the engine that day (August 16, 1914) not to tell anyone at the Meadows how easy it was to keep up steam on an E6, or firemen with more seniority would bid in on the run and "bump" him off the job. Pennsy men used to say you could put a lighted candle in each corner of an empty firebox of an E6s and generate enough steam to take a train over a Division. That is what they thought of those Atlantics!

Back on the Meadows after bringing in No. 56 from Washington, Lee and Garrett relax for a moment before proceeding to the inspection pit.

Engine 737 has just completed a run well over 200 miles from Washington, D.C. Her engine crew Martin Lee and Joe Garrett, obligingly pose for the camera while Charles B. Chaney stands between them. To the right can be seen the embankment of the Pennsy's "high-line" on which the DD1 motors took passengers directly into New York City without changing trains.

Martin Lee's favorite E6s, No. 779. With this engine Lee covered the 35.7 miles from Washington to Loudon Park in 25 minutes when hauling a nine car train. Reading from left to right, we have, Charley Chaney, Martin Lee, third man is unknown, and on extreme right a top-notch fireman, Joe Garrett. Engine is on the ready track all set to run to the Transfer, and take No. 59, the Congressional Limited to Washington.

No. 779 topping the grade at Loudon Park, Maryland. As usual Joe Garrett has a good head of steam in the boiler and engineman Lee has the heavy 11 car train well in hand. This was train 92, in September 1914. No. 779 was the last engine he ever drove.

Chapter 10
Oliver P. Keller (1905—1925)

This is one of the most complete pictorial records of the career of a Pennsy locomotive engineer during the time he spent on engines hauling the road's top-name trains. Chief among these was the Pennsylvania Special which in 1912 became the Broadway Limited. The illustrations cover twenty years of Keller's train operating activities at the throttle from 1905 to 1925.

It also progressively represents Pennsy passenger locomotive development on the road east of Pittsburgh from the days of the light Atlantics to the mighty K4s class Pacifics.

Oliver O. Keller was born in 1855, and early in his youth began working for the Pennsylvania Railroad at Harrisburg. Soon he became a locomotive fireman, and through the arduous stages of switching, freight and passenger service, he achieved his ambition by becoming a passenger locomotive engineer on the Philadelphia Division. By 1904, Keller was hauling trains between Broad Street Station and Harrisburg, Pa. When the New York-Pittsburgh subway, or Mantua tunnel, was opened in December 1904, he began running trains between Harrisburg, and Jersey City. He was one of three Philadelphia Division engineers from Harrisburg who first ran the revived Pennsylvania Special after it had been discontinued in February 1904 due to a freight traffic blockade in the Pittsburgh region. But construction of the "Brilliant Branch" which permitted much freight traffic to bypass the congested area substantially relieved the situation. This had much to do in re-establishing the Pennsylvania Special, and cutting its running time to 18 hours between New York and Chicago.

Three engineers who handled train 28, the eastbound section of the Special, were Jim Brady, George Ewing, and Ollie Keller, in that order of seniority. Brady took the train from Harrisburg to Jersey City, on its first eastbound run on the 18 hour schedule, and though the schedule called for an average speed of about 60 mph he made it easily. He had engine No. 1610, an E3a built at Juniata in 1904.

The engineers on this run had one day on and two days off, thus when Keller took No. 28 east, say on a Monday morning, he did not work this train until the following Thursday. The return westbound run was made with the same engine used with train 28, but with train No. 17, the Western Adams Express, which arrived at Harrisburg early the next morning. Train 17, left Jersey City, at 9:22 p.m., and as the Special arrived at Jersey City that same morning, it gave a longer layover than the crews liked in general. For train 28 had an excellent record for punctuality, and that meant about twelve hours of daylight layover time. Later this time was cut to a shorter layover period, as the engine crews insisted that they were able to get enough rest to make the return run to Harrisburg easily. In fact, when engine crews began running a longer distance between Jersey City and Washington, D.C., the men had shorter layover time, yet in a most capable manner performed their duties.

Ollie Keller had a brother named Frank, who like himself was a Philadelphia Division engineman. Frank Keller drove train No. 5, the Pennsylvania Limited between Broad Street Station and Harrisburg, regularly before his retirement which preceded that of his brother Oliver. Both men between them served the Pennsy for over a century. Ollie Keller lived for 18 years after his mandatory retirement at age 70, reaching the ripe old age of 88 years.

Engine 1610 pulled the first eastbound section of the revived Pennsylvania Special in June 1905 between Harrisburg and Jersey City. The distance of 189 miles was regularly covered in 196 minutes, at an average speed of 57.7 mph. Here we see Ollie Keller on train No. 28, the eastbound section of the Pennsylvania Special, passing "3" office tower with the regular five car consist. No postal car was carried by this train during the wooden car era or for some time after the all-steel cars appeared. But 18 feet of space was contracted for by the United States Railway Mail Service, and alotted for the use of a railway post office clerk at the front end of the combination car.

The eastbound Pennsy Special with a clear stack has just crossed the Delaware River on track No. 1, and passed a much slower moving freight train on Track No. 2. Engine 1610 built in 1904 at Juniata, has the older style wooden "long" pilot, as it heads No. 28. The fireman is giving a friendly wave to the photographer as the train enters New Jersey. That long stone bridge separating Pennsylvania from New Jersey, was opened for traffic on September 13, 1903. Date of this scene was in the year 1906.

One of the earlier Atlantics, engine 1973, class E2, with its round-top firebox roof sheet eastbound to Jersey City with train 28. Ollie Keller at the throttle. Train has just crossed the Schuylkill River and is approaching "BX" tower.

A close-up of No. 151 at North Philadelphia in 1908. Ollie Keller and George Z. Gray, fireman. Gray told me that this was a fine engine until it had a sideswipe somewhere on the Philadelphia Division. After that, he said, the engine just was no good; it seemed to have gotten a "twist" in it, rode roughly, and would not steam. No. 151 has the newer and shorter pilot. Main brake pipe and air signal pipe are above pilot beam as was customary on most Pennsy passenger locomotives. The pilot beam was made of white oak.

Another good E3a class engine was No. 2066. Train is passing the Philadelphia Zoo alongside road to the left. Engine was built at Juniata in 1905, and train 28 has the normal five car consist in order from engine as follows:

    Pullman Parlor Smoking Car, Chicago to New York
    Pennsylvania RR. Dining Car, Chicago to Alliance-Harrisburg to New York
    Pullman Drawing room State-Room Sleeping Cars, (2) Chicago to New York
    Pullman Observation Compartment Car, Chicago to New York

As noted above, train is passing the Zoo, and today a large interlocking tower in this vicinity is appropriately enough called "Zoo Tower."

One of the first engines assigned to train 28, was E3a class engine No. 151 built at Juniata in 1905. On this day the train seems to be one car short with only four cars instead of the usual five. Perhaps the Cincinnati connection was too late at Pittsburgh to couple up with No. 28.

A good close-up of 1973 at North Philadelphia in 1907. Engine crew was Keller and George Gray. Conductor at rear of tender was Harry Leonard. This engine was assigned to the Special for some time. It ran east with train 28, and came back to Harrisburg with train No. 17, the Western Adams Express, which left Jersey City at 9:22 p.m. Both engine and train crew were from Harrisburg and returned west on No. 17. Engine 1973 is the same class that engineer Jerry McCarthy of Lines West, reputedly made 127.1 mph with the Pennsy Special in 1905, and engine 7002. There were only four tracks—all main line—at North Philadelphia Station in 1907. Originally named Germantown Junction, it was renamed in 1904. By 1914 platforms of the raised island type were installed and more trackage added.

A speed shot takes in 1907 of engine No. 374, class E3a built in 1905. Keller is waving at the photographer, his friend John S. Powell, while Gray looks on from the gangway. Train is the Pennsylvania Special, No. 28, and Keller later told Powell, that he was making 80 mph when this picture was taken. This engine was Keller's favorite light Atlantic, and Gray told me that it was a fine "steamer" and the speediest of all the light Atlantics in both their experience. Train is approaching Andalusia, Pa.

Class E2d engine No. 3136 built in 1906, at North Philadelphia, with the eastbound Pennsylvania Special. On these engines as on class E3d, the saddle was an individual casting while the cylinders and piston valves on each side were separate castings, making three castings in all. Before 1910, all light Atlantics were built with spoked forward truck wheels.

Engine 374 on the tangent track after rounding the Torresdale curve. Keller is leaning far out of the cab window in an effort to get into the picture. Even in those long by-gone days of 1907 you can see that the Pennsy was a four-tracked main line well ballasted and neatly fenced in. Train is passing Andalusia, Pa.

A close-up of engine No. 2066 at North Philadelphia, with Keller and fireman Gray on the job. Steam heat is being used as can be seen by the steam between engine tender and combination car. The dark blue cap on the baggagemaster indicates that the picture was taken between October and May, when winter uniforms were used. White caps were used with lighter weight summer uniforms that were worn between May and October. An interesting item is the location of the main brake and signal pipes that are placed under the pilot beam. On most Pennsy locomotives they were on top of the beam, thereby conforming to usual practice.

Engine 2019 of the E3 class, built in 1902. This class was rarely seen on this part of the Pennsy where train 29 is climbing the grade between Narberth and Wynnewood, Pa. Ollie Keller is at the throttle and waving to the photographer. The second car was a steel dining car, class D70, but the rest of the cars, all Pullman, were of wooden construction. This again, is a case of where they were beginning to sandwich steel cars into the train in the year 1909, when this picture was taken. This was the class of locomotive designed for the Pittsburgh Division and first built in 1901. Engine still retained old long pilot, cinder chute and slide. With more tractive force the E3, and its subclasses were favored by the Philadelphia and Pittsburgh Divisions, where this extra muscle could be used to advantage.

A big non-superheated K2 class Pacific No. 997, built in 1910, is hauling the Pennsylvania Special in 1911, as Keller passes Andalusia, Pa. Those big 16-inch piston valves weighed 263 pounds, but were later replaced by a 12 inch valve that only weighed 120 pounds. Each side of the steam dome had a safety valve; this was a standard feature on most of the early K2 class engines east of Pittsburgh. Later they were placed on the roof sheet of the firebox where some were enclosed in a casing and some were not.

Ollie Keller at the right, and conductor Harry Leonard at the left as they stop for a bit at North Philadelphia with the Pennsylvania Special in 1911. Engine was 3337, a class K2 assigned to the Philadelphia Division.

For awhile Keller was assigned to train No. 40, the Cincinnati Express, during 1912 and 1913. Engine is a K2 Pacific No. 3342, hauling a train made up of all-steel coaches, Pullmans and dining car. Train is passing "BX" interlocking tower, the first one east of the Schuylkill River bridge and was then on the New York Division where the train dispatchers in Jersey City were in charge of train operation.

A good view of a typical bracket post signal structure that governed train movements between Overbrook and Paoli. The Pennsylvania Special in 1911, has just passed a Paoli local at Narberth Station. Train 29 is running the inside No. 3 freight track, and the bracket post signals give both trains a clear track. The bulky K2 with Ollie Keller at the throttle is rapidly taking advantage of the situation, and with those 24″ × 26″ cylinders powering those 80 inch drivers, engine No. 3337 is picking up speed as it climbs uphill.

Engine 3373, class K2, on the short two-tracked section between Girard Avenue, and "BX" tower. Engine was built in 1911, but unlike light Atlantics, cylinders and valve chests on the K2 locomotives were cast in two half saddles and bolted in the center. Keller and George Gray are the engine crew.

Coming up from the New York-Pittsburgh subway tunnel, K2 engine 3370, built in 1911, wheels train No. 40, on its way between Harrisburg and New York. Train is passing "3" tower in West Philadelphia. The K2 was cut off at Manhattan Transfer where a 4,000 horsepower DD1 class electric locomotive took the train 8.8 miles over the Jersey meadows, under hilly Weehawken and the Hudson River tunnels to Penn Station on Manhattan Island. Engineman Keller and fireman Gray on the job.

Train 29, the Pennsylvania Special with K2, No. 3373, approaching the Torresdale reverse curve with its regular six-car consist of those days. The all-steel Pullmans had sides of simulated wooden tongue and groove boards. This was done to allay the fears of passengers who erroneously dreaded electrocution during a thunder and lightning storm. The dining car, however, had smooth sides and was a Pennsy owned and operated car. Train make-up which had been consistent since 1910 was a Combination Car, Dining Car, three Sleeping Cars, and one Observation Compartment Sleeping Car with a metal railing enclosing an open platform. Photo was taken April 20, 1912.

A heavy load for E3a class engine No. 1601 built in 1903. They must have been short of K2 Pacifics, and Keller got a light Atlantic to handle train No. 40 that day. It was made up of all-steel equipment and date was probably 1911. Although the train is made up of nine cars it is proceeding at a right smart pace. Fireman Gray told me that 1601 was a real good locomotive, as compared to some others of the same class.

Another picture of K2 No. 3373, hauling the Pennsylvania Special in 1912, as it passes Andalusia, Pa., on track No. 2, the eastbound freight track. It can be seen that some changes have taken place on this engine as compared to the other picture of this same No. 3373. It had in the meanwhile been equipped with a superheater in October 1912, as indicated by the superheater damper's counterweight just above the running board in back of the smokebox. The auxiliary dome casing of the safety valves had been removed, and instead of steps supported from the running boards, new steps forming part of the front valve chest cover have replaced them. Note the slot in the lever and quadrant operated reach rod located almost in mid-gear under the front of the air drum. That and the large tank of coal still left after leaving Harrisburg, well over 100 miles distant, shows the economy of operating on a short cut-off and full throttle.

The most advanced design of the K2 Pacifics. Engine No. 3402, class K2sa, built in 1912, at the head end of the Manhattan Limited train 22, in 1913. Stones at the right were for construction of the stone arch bridge that replaced the truss. Two large arches with widened additions to the smaller arches, supported five main line tracks. All were in full operation by 1914. Engine 3402 was built at Juniata as a superheated locomotive. The main air drum, or reservoir on the right-hand side was moved ahead of the firebox, but did not change its location on the left-hand side. Due to its higher tender deck, for it was intended to stoker fire these locomotives, the cab roof was cut away closer to the rain gutter on the cab roof. Outside steam pipes fed steam to the valve chests. This engine used the screw reverse handwheel arrangement to actuate the reach rod which the men preferred to the former lever and quadrant method for reversing the locomotive. For some time Keller had train 22 eastbound and went west to Harrisburg on No. 29, the Broadway Limited.

Oliver Keller at the throttle of No. 1794, the first E6s built in 1914. Train is No. 22, the Eastbound Manhattan Limited from Chicago to New York. The featured "KW" trailing truck with a side frame that also served as an equalizing beam between the rear drivers and the trailing truck, had two openings per side to reduce weight in the side frames. No other E6s locomotive built in 1914 appears to have had these attempts at weight reduction. Later, two coil springs were placed under the trailing trucks two axle boxes to further improve the riding quality of these generally smooth riding engines. Train was moving over 70 mph when picture was taken in 1914. Location was Eddington, Pa., station, on the New York Division.

Engine 1397, hauling the Manhattan Limited bound for New York in 1914. Train had just rounded the Torresdale reverse curve and is straightening out on a long tangent as it passes Andalusia, Pa. on the New York Division. Oliver Keller is at the throttle and with an all-steel car train of ten cars is easily maintaining a steady speed of 70 mph. While Keller considered the E6s a good engine, the rugged westbound run on the Philadelphia Division made the going rough at times with a four-coupled Atlantic. Thus when the six-coupled class K4s came on the scene, as far as he was concerned, the E6s was not in it. On the other hand, engineman Martin Lee, who never had the chance to run a K4 between Manhattan Transfer and Washington, D.C., thought the E6s Atlantics the best passenger engines the Pennsy ever operated. Gradient profile conditions between these two points may well have contributed to Mr. Lee's opinion in this respect.

This was a publicity shot of the Broadway Limited taken in September 1920, and shows the kind of engine Keller was driving at the time. Picture was taken at Cornwells, Pa., (now Cornwells Heights) opposite Michells Seed Gardens, and close to Cornwells interlocking tower, known as "CO" and long since removed. Engine was No. 3758 of the K4s class built in 1920. This scene appeared in the Pennsy public timetables for some years, and obviously had some air brush work done on the surrounding scenery and the locomotive. What is puzzling is the fact that the locomotive does not have piston tail rods. At that time the K4's did have them, and they were applied on newly built engines of this class as late as 1924. It is doubtful if this engine was operating without tail rods at this time, for if so, results between then and 1924 would have been determined long before if it were an experimental procedure. On these engines, all built in 1920 (3726-3775 series) new tenders with high tank collars replaced the low-sided 70-P-70 class. The new tenders were known as class 70-P-70a. First three Pullmans from engine were named, Export, Baldwin, and Frazer. Nine car consist with one dining car was the standard make-up in 1920.

In July 1924, Keller wheels the Broadway Limited around the curve approaching Cornwells. Engine was 3763, class K4s, Juniata built. Due to use of the screw reverse, the cab was shortened considerably. To cover the screw reverse at the front end a small metal protrusion outside the cab and right under the front window was used. This engine has extended piston rod guides or tail rods, and was equipped with them when built, yet the picture was taken in July 1924. A round-case headlight has supplanted the square-case older style originally applied to these 3700 series when built as can be seen on No. 3758. The square-ended upper quadrant semi-automatic home semaphore controlled from "CO" interlocking tower, is dropping to stop position on westbound track No. 4. Signals on eastbound tracks 1 and 2, are single-bladed pointed-end automatics, actuated by the trains.

Another 1924 photo of a K4 as it waits on the ready track at the Meadows enginehouse. Shortly after No. 1980, built at Juniata in 1918, headed for the steam storage track at the west end of Manhattan Transfer where it waited for The Broadway. In back of the outside steam pipe on both sides the superheater damper counterweight was lowered, thereby closing it by gravity. When the throttle was opened steam actuated the counterweight mechanism and raised it a bit over a horizontal position thus opening the damper. Later, in view of improved superheater construction, dampers were no longer considered a necessity, and their omission on K4's was later noticeable as they were altered to suit newer conditions. The steam powered device and counterweights were no longer used; in fact some of the last batch of newly built K4s class engines did not have them. On the deck of the low-sided 70-P-70 class tender stood Ollie Keller, veteran engineer of this train since 1905, when it was called the Pennsylvania Special. Fireman Gearhart, I understand, rests on the seatbox. This engine has the smokebox front held to the internal ring with symmetrically spaced bolts above and below the centerline. It is also apparent that the bottom of the plate has warped, and why, on the latest K4's Pennsy doubled the bolts under the centerline to impart greater rigidity at this "smokebox crinkle" zone.

The Broadway Limited was really rolling as it passed Andalusia, Pa., this day in 1925. Engine 3881 was a K4s built at Juniata in 1923, and was one of the engines assigned to the Broadway. Engines of the 3800 group were the first K4's to be equipped with power reverse gears, and round-cased headlights. Another acquisition was a new tender known as class 70-P-70d. Still retained from earlier days were the piston tail rods, crosshead and guides, rim stack smoke lifter, and safety strap at the end of the guides. Train was passing Andalusia, Pa., on its westbound trek to Chicago. Ollie Keller is waving to his good friend John Powell, who by means of his fine photographic skill gave us an illustrative biographical record of this fine locomotive engineer.

REPORT OF CARS ON PASSENGER TRAIN

(A) To_____ (B) From New York (C) Oct. 20th 192 3

(D) _____ Sec. of (F) 29 Arr. (G) _____ M. Left (H) _____ X _____ M.

(J) Engine 3881 with Cars in following order from Engine

	Kind of Car (K)	Number or Name of Car (M)	Point of Origin (N)	Final Destination (O)
1	PC	9767	New York	Chicago
2	PLR.	Maple Shade	"	"
3	Sl.231	Ronk	"	"
4	" 7	Vemonder	"	"
5	" 29	Thespis	"	"
6	" 6	Hiconder	"	"
7	Dn.	4489	"	Altoona
8	Sl.30	Diogenes	"	Chicago
9	" 31	LaVergne	"	"
10	Cb.32	Carpenter	"	"
11				
12	Electric Engine #14			
13	Engineman Tobin			
14	Helper Westfall			
15				
16				
P	Total Number of Cars 10 cars			

(Q) Conductor H.Leonard (R) Engineman O.P.Keller

(S) Baggage Master L.Mowery (U) Fireman J.N.Shindler

(V) Brakemen J.Fentzer

(W) Train Crew went on duty 255a M (X) Must be relieved prior to 1255a M

(Y) Engine Crew went on duty 50-a M (Z) Must be relieved prior to _____ M

(AB) Individual members of train or engine crew excepted in above ordering and relieving time as follows:- _____

C&B Respited 4 hrs and 20 mins.

Bag " 4 "

Bkm. on 16 Mxt. 5:45 A.M.

(AC) Remarks _____

Sleeper Ronk off

_____

_____

(**B) _____ Superintendent

it be forwarded to eparture of each train.

This is a copy of the CT 220 report which represented a listing of the actual train consist and crew members. It is an authentic record of the westbound Broadway Limited on October 20, 1923, when headed by engine 3881 when driven by Ollie Keller. Also recorded is the DD1 motor No. 14 that hauled the train to Manhattan Transfer, and its engine crew comprising engineman Tobin, and helper Westfall.

Taken shortly before Keller's retirement in 1925. Train was approaching the Torresdale reverse curve and hauling twelve steel cars. Ten were heavy-weight Pullmans rated at 85 tons each, and two were dining cars weighing 90 tons each, giving a total train weight of 1,030 tons, exclusive of engine and tender. The enormous power of superheated steam is obvious when we consider the fact that just two cylinders and three pairs of drivers are propelling this great weight. The engine No. 5375, built at Juniata in 1924, was Keller's favorite K4, and he informed Powell that he was hitting 80 mph when this picture was taken. Heavy drag of axle-driven generators (one per car) for charging their weighty batteries, plus steam for train heating (in season) hot water for the shower bath and use of the barber in the Parlor Baggage car, and steam tables in the dining cars; all this from one steam locomotive that cost about one-fifth the price of one diesel unit which could not haul this train at the same speed. Now a single-unit electric locomotive; but that is a different story! Tender was class 70-P-70d, and see how the superheater counterweight has risen with an open throttle.

Epilogue

It has always seemed to this writer that the Pennsylvania Railroad during Theodore N. Ely's tenure of office had a "small engine" policy. That is they used the smallest and lightest locomotives consistent with traffic requirements.

Economically this made sense for it permitted construction of a comparatively low cost locomotive. With fewer parts to inspect and maintain, operating costs were cut substantially. Compared with engines on railroads using six-coupled wheel arrangements, Ely's superb American and Atlantic types made this cost reduction quite evident.

And for another point, it is always desirable to reduce machine friction; locomotive rail adhesion excepted. The Pennsy's retention, therefore, of the four-coupled wheel format was sound. Obviously there was a decrease in moving parts on a locomotive with four driving wheels compared to one with six.

The old London & North Western and Midland Railways of Great Britain, pursued this "small engine" policy, and in their day were probably the most solvent of British Railways. But as trains became longer and heavier double-heading became necessary. This was quite prevalent and costly on the L&NW Rwy., in the days of Francis W. Webb's regime as Locomotive Chief, though his controversial compounds played a part in this situation. The Midland got around the doubleheading problem by cutting train lengths and running more of them headed by one locomotive. This action was appreciated by the traveling public, as it provided more frequent service to locations on their line, but as with doubleheading it did increase operating costs.

Even the Pennsy with their penchant for the four-coupled type were confronted with the problem of heavier trains. A steady infiltration from 1907 on of all-steel car particularly on the road east of Pittsburgh forced them to the class K2 Pacific.

Although class K2 was doing well with increasingly heavier trains, Ely viewed them somewhat tolerantly and apparently evinced no enthusiasm for the Pacifics. His desire to retain the four-coupled engine concept gave Alfred W. Gibbs, the support of his Chief in the development of his super Atlantics of class E6s. Four-coupled engines for passenger service and sturdy reliable 2-8-0 type Consolidations for freight service; a winning team, why change?

In March 1920, James T. Wallis became Chief of Motive Power of the whole Pennsylvania Railroad System, at Pennsy headquarters in Broad Street Station, Philadelphia. He recognized the need for greater power in freight and passenger service locomotives. Taking some ingredients from Alco's giant K29s class Pacific, and the Pennsy's latest E6s design of 1914, Wallis produced a Pacific of Pacifics, class K4s in 1914. Just before the Pacific came a Mikado from Juniata's erecting shop. Even then the Pennsy were showing a conservative approach, for both heavier Pacifics and Mikados had been on other roads many years before 1914. In fact, some railroads had already gone to the Mountain and Santa Fe types for Passenger and freight service respectively. The Pennsy were again keeping to well known wheel arrangements and were surpassed in weight and power by similar types elsewhere. Neither did they go to the Hudson type which many regard as the peak of the six-coupled wheel arrangement for high-speed passenger service. The Santa Fe type did get on the road around 1919, but again was a latecomer, and Mallets in small number, made "one shot" appearances. My reference to a "small engine" policy is aimed at the standard types that appeared in large quantity in the period stated from the 1890's to designs before 1920.

It does, therefore, seem reasonable and interesting to consider the belief that the Pennsy preferred the comparatively small or at best moderately heavy type locomotive of a specific class (except the E6s class) capable of doing the job. In this they were not unlike their British Railway counterparts previously referred to in their use of a "small engine" policy — in the period covered by this book.

END

Frederick Westing

Acknowledgments

Much of the information in this book is due to conversations and correspondence with former employes of the Pennsylvania Railroad. Many worked in an official capacity and others were men who fired and drove Pennsy steam locomotives in the days before Penn Station was opened.

Access to personal records kept of their runs on the road and informally written notes contained authentic information that never found its way into the technical press of the day, or even the authoritative Pennsy Test Plant Bulletins.

Miss Elvira Ferguson, Librarian of the now defunct Pennsy Library, most kindly permitted me to delve into the voluminous railroad lore reposing there. This included the railroad's old "Day Book" wherein were kept minutes of the Board of Directors meetings, and other records of high officials of the road. It was kept by the railroad's Secretary when the Pennsy was "Number One" among railroads.

To my wife Margaret, and our friend Mrs. Regina Curry, who helped greatly in checking the numerous galley proofs of text and captions, I am most grateful.

Credit for certain information is given in the text to those who supplied it, but to the many engine crews, and shop men I spoke to at various localities and not known to me by name, my sincere gratitude. Fortunately I was able in some instances to supply these gentlemen with booklets, manuals, and pamphlets covering diesel-electric locomotive operation, which they told me was of much help to them. In this way I was glad to make some substantial return for their kindness. For by that time the diesel was definitely in the picture.

Let all who may enjoy this book give thanks to those gracious folks who enabled me — as they say these days — "to put it all together."

Frederick Westing

Index